GOD

ADAM & EVE

WORSHIP

SIN

SPIRITUAL WIDOWHOOD

THE PROMISE

THE BRIDEGROOM

DELIVERANCE

BETHROTHAL

REDEMPTION

MARRIAGE

RESTORATION

Andy Mendonsa

WESTBOW
PRESS®
A DIVISION OF THOMAS NELSON
& ZONDERVAN

Scripture quotations marked KJV are from the Holy Bible, King James Version (Authorized Version). First published in 1611. Quoted from the KJV Classic Reference Bible, Copyright © 1983 by The Zondervan Corporation.

WestBow Press books may be ordered through booksellers or by contacting:

WestBow Press
A Division of Thomas Nelson & Zondervan
1663 Liberty Drive
Bloomington, IN 47403
www.westbowpress.com
1 (866) 928-1240

ISBN: 978-1-5127-6844-2 (sc)
ISBN: 978-1-5127-6845-9 (hc)
ISBN: 978-1-5127-6843-5 (e)

Library of Congress Control Number: 2016920752

Print information available on the last page.

WestBow Press rev. date: 02/20/2017

Our daughter, Hadrienne Kathleen Mendonsa
and our son, Asher River Mendonsa

Spiritual Widowhood is dedicated to the memory of our daughter, Hadrienne Kathleen Mendonsa (December 30, 1985–November 19, 2005), and our son, Asher River Mendonsa, aka Asher Love (December 22, 1987–April 21, 2015).

The following quotation was taken from a letter Hadrienne wrote when she was just seventeen to one of her high school teachers, Forrest Walker. She never mailed the letter, though, and it wasn't discovered until after she was tragically, and unexpectedly, taken from my wife and I. This written but unsent letter was in response to this teacher's act of kindness our daughter observed. It was not an act that would have been noticed if he had not done it, nor would it have been noticed by anyone except the person it was intended for. Hadrienne noticed. And she was so moved by this seemingly insignificant act of kindness that she revealed her own struggles in carrying out similar acts of kindness based on Jesus's own words and life example. The excerpt is as follows:

> I have become all too aware of intentions turning into choices. Too often my intentions fall into a choice to ignore rather than to act. As Jesus showed us, we are to love all, no matter the recognition we get, no matter the situation. We are to go the extra mile to show love, and not just to intend to show love.

Table of Contents

Foreword

"Thank you, Lord, for another day to wake up and praise your name." That seemingly simple prayer has been the most important thing I've learned from many of the widows at Widows Harvest Ministries' lunch-hour prayer meetings on Tuesdays. It's funny—well, maybe not so funny—that I've always taken the normal beauty, and the opportunity and the gift, of another day for granted. I just assume that I am going to wake up, take a shower, drink some coffee, drive to work, work a few hours, return home, and go back to bed, just to wake up again the next day. Sure, I'll mix in some fun with my family and with coworkers, or maybe it'll be a weekend so I'll watch my kids play soccer and then go to church with my friends. But I always assume—better yet, presume—that another day is owed to me. This presumption impacts the way I live my life. The implications are many: what I stress out about, how I use my time, and how I treat others being just a few. But perhaps the most important lesson I've learned from the widows' prayers is the lesson of gratitude. They are grateful to their Creator and Sustainer for the opportunity to get up one more time and walk with him again. Yes, there are many challenges that they have and offer prayers about: family, health, money, sadness, loss, violence, and yes, they cry when they pray, but they also sing and dance. I've learned so much from these spiritual mothers.

In addition to being blessed by the widows of WHM, the other blessing I have received is Andy Mendonsa's friendship, the Director of this Ministry. Andy and I have had lunch almost weekly since 2013. I first met him when I worked for a local church here in Chattanooga and I came and shared the vision and ministry of and for widows to an out-of-town church group looking for a mission's experience to serve in the inner city. Little did I know then that a few years later I would be having regular meetings with Andy because of my new work with a local Christian foundation. Over these lunches, I've gotten to know Andy and to love him as a friend. I've also learned a lot of the history of our city, Chattanooga, and of its many inner-city ministries over the years. He's told me how he stumbled into widows' ministry when meeting a widow who needed home repairs. And over the next thirty years, these widows and many others have taught him to understand his own relationship with Jesus in light of our human condition of widowhood.

Andy has been on this journey for several decades. He's now invited me to wrestle with what God's Word says about the widow and the orphan, our relationship to them and to him, and how worship is to be shaped by our understanding of our own condition of widowhood. I will admit, and so will Andy, that as men we have much to learn from these mothers. It may not always be easy to understand or fully grasp the implications of our own condition and how that impacts our worship, but Andy has been patient with and kind to me, just as I'm sure the widows have been patient and kind with him as he's wrestled with this matter—and just like the Lord has been patient and kind with the widows as they've had to learn to thank him as he's walked with them amid the major life change that brought them to be widows.

Andy now invites you on this journey as well. Here he challenges us to wrestle with what the Lord meant by "religion that is pure and undefiled before God the Father is this: to visit orphans and widows in their affliction, and to keep oneself unstained from the world" (James 1:27 ESV). You may not feel all that comfortable as you read. And, as you may have questions or find that you may not agree, you can always invite Andy out for a burger and good conversation. I'm certain he will be patient and kind with you, too.

Thank you, Andy, for your friendship.
Eduardo Centurion

Acknowledgments

Gloria Mendonsa, my wife of thirty-two years, has taught me what it means to love and be loved unconditionally, even though I fall short of the latter every single day. When it comes to love, actions do speak louder than words. Gloria has also demonstrated for me what it looks like to be a bride, and not just in the easy times, but also through unimaginable tragedy, such as when we first lost our daughter, Hadrienne, and then our son, Asher.

I also acknowledge Beverly Glover Jackson, my mother, who had a difficult pregnancy with me and was required to stay in bed for most of it, being allowed to get up only one hour a day. Having had a miscarriage with her previous pregnancy, she spent much of her time praying that God would allow me to be born. For my whole life, she has maintained that she named me Andrew because of a dream she had one night during the time before I was born. When I was older, she prayed and fasted on my behalf for almost a year before I finally submitted to God's call for my life, six months before my twenty-seventh birthday. Even before she became a widow herself for the second time (after my parents divorced and her second husband passed away), she was involved with the prayer ministry of widows, teaching the weekly Bible study for years. Now each week she joins the other widows who are involved in our widows' prayer ministry to pray with them.

The Late Arthur A. (Don) Mendonsa, my father, set a very high bar for honesty and integrity that I remain eternally grateful for. With my father having been the City Manager of Savannah, Georgia, for twenty-eight years, I was able to observe him firsthand in leading a life without compromising his integrity or the things he strongly believed in, especially when it came to ensuring the equitable treatment of all of Savannah's citizens by local government. Then, late in his career, using his position as City Manager, he obsessively pursued what would later become, along with the help of other equally concerned citizens, including future Mayor of Savannah, Otis Johnson, a nonprofit in Savannah called Youth Futures. Not only was my father greatly burdened for helping at-risk youth succeed, but also he had a particular concern for the high mortality rate of low-income African American teen mothers. This burden not only helped lead to the establishment of Youth Futures but also led the state of Georgia to hire my father to write a planning manual through the University of Georgia's Carl Vinson Institute of Government that was, in turn, adopted by the state to be used to implement similar strategies for helping youth at risk in cities and towns throughout the state. The title of this manual is "Helping Children Become Successful Adults: A Planning Manual for Communities." Tragically, my father was killed in 1999 while hiking out in Colorado. He slipped and fell sixty feet, and later died at Mercy Hospital in the city of Durango.

I also acknowledge the late Robert Reid Kalley, an independent Scottish missionary who went to the Madeira Islands in 1838 and started a mission there. Both sets of parents of my great-grandparents were among his thousands of converts, who would, by necessity, immigrate to America in the 1850s as part of a larger group of two thousand who have come to be known as the Portuguese Exiles. These exiles were given land in Jacksonville, Illinois, where they all came and settled and established a Portuguese Presbyterian church. Growing up, I had heard vague details about these exiles and about the possibility of our family having been among them, but it wasn't until a few years ago that I found a biography of Robert Reid Kalley's life called *The Wolf from Scotland* and learned the true story of how our family had to flee from Madeira to escape religious persecution and came to settle in Jacksonville, Illinois. My great-grandparents were Emanuel L. Mendonsa and Julia V. Mendonsa. Their parents who came over were

Emanuel Mendonsa and Mary Mendonsa and Joseph P. Correa and Mary Vincent Correa respectively.

I acknowledge the late Gertrude Gaston, who became my prayer partner, and whom I consider to be the cofounder of the ministry for widows we started in 1987. When Mrs. Gaston's husband, Marion, died, she prayed that God would keep her so busy ministering to others that she wouldn't have time to grieve or mourn. Gertrude devoted every day to praying and serving God. She wouldn't have a TV or even a radio in her house because she didn't want any distractions from her time with the Lord. More days than not, both men and women would come to her house for prayer, especially for troubled marriages. She was responsible for the prayer ministry of widows that has become the focus of Widows Harvest.

I acknowledge the late Harry Davis and his wife, Catherine, my uncle and aunt, who gave me refuge in December of 1982 after coming back from Germany with no money or a place to live after failing to find a job there. It was shortly after my return, while living with them, that I surrendered my life to serving God.

I also thank Pastor George Thompson, my first pastor, who may be the most loving and kind person I have ever met and who showed me what a pastor who truly has the gift and calling to be a pastor looks like.

Also on my list of people to acknowledge are Leland Stewart, Mark Mollenkof, and Gary Hellriegel, who believed in this ministry to widows and, in effect, believed in me. I hope they know how instrumental they were in helping me to start the ministry. I want each of them to know that I have never forgotten and my gratitude is eternal.

Dr. Evelyn Polite, founder and director of Widows Harvest Savannah (Georgia), remains an inspiration to me. At age sixty-eight, when most believers are thinking about retirement, Dr. Polite founded Widows Harvest Savannah and has been faithfully leading and directing this ministry to widows in Savannah ever since.

The late Tommy Haymes, my dear friend, Widows Harvest Ministries board chairman, and brother of brothers in the Lord, is a man I miss. I am not certain how the ministry has continued on since the Lord took him to the place he had prepared for him in his presence.

I also thank Larry Reed and Luz Hernandez. Larry served as the first chairman of Widows Harvest Ministries (WHM), and Luz served as treasurer of WHM and then later stepped in and served as interim chairwoman after our dear friend and brother Tommy Haymes passed away. Both Larry and Luz, at critical times in the history of WHM, faithfully served. Words cannot properly express my gratitude for both of them.

With special gratitude, I thank Lisa Eames, my assistant and Administrator for Widows Harvest Ministries, who, without her commitment, organizational skills, leadership abilities and extraordinary levels of patience this ministry would not be what it is today.

Deeply grateful for Dick Mason and his invaluable service and contributions to Widows Harvest through his seemingly tireless efforts to meet the home repair needs on widow's homes for over 20 years.

I acknowledge Reverend Gene Yelverton, my prayer partner for the summer and only time I was enrolled for classes at Asbury Seminary. His wisdom and his patience with me came at such a crucial time in my life. He taught me about prayer and waiting on God for the answer. The analogy he gave me about prayer being answered was that it is like a baseball game starting. The game can't be started until all of the players are on the field. When we pray, God is the one that then arranges everyone and everything as he wants it to be before the answer comes. Not only are the choicest of fruits produced in this way, but he also gets all of the credit. Often, in our haste and impatience, though, we want to force our prayers to be answered by arranging circumstances of our choosing, which only seems to produce fruit that is neither choice or long lasting and quickly dies on the vine before it has a chance to reproduce itself.

With the utmost regard for Servant Pastor Joshua Atieno and his wife, Abigael Atieno, who started Widows Harvest Africa in 2004 and have faithfully served as its Directors ever since. Based in Miwani, Kenya, this ministry not only provides much needed assistance to widows in the region with both housing and food needs, but they have also built a widow's ministry center named the "Hadrienne Kathleen Mendonsa Widow's Ministry and Prayer Center in memory of our daughter and dedicated in 2006. One of the primary purposes of this center is as a place where widows can regularly gather for prayer and fasting. Often for 24 hours a day, with widows each praying in 8 hour shifts, when dire needs arise calling for such fervent prayer.

The late Brother Eugene Gizzi, a vowed member of the Alexian Brothers, who among his many accomplishments throughout his life of service to the Lord pioneered the establishment of the Alexian Brothers in the Philippines, is a man I was proud to call my adopted father.

Very thankful for my friend Dr. Carl Ellis Jr. who, for many years, through many a lunch-time conversation over either Chinese or Indian food, most patiently allowed me to bounce theological insights and ideas that I was wrestling with at the time. I am especially thankful to him for his insights into the minority/cross cultural dynamic that existed in Acts 6:1-7 that he first brought to my attention several years ago, and something that will be discussed in Chapter 18.

I thank Dr. Rick Sharp for the insight he gave to me for the third cup at the Last Supper during the Passover meal, something that will be discussed in greater depth in Chapter 16.

A special thanks to Moriah Bond. I had been trying for over five years to write this book but after attempting to do so multiple times I had almost given up when I received a letter in the mail from Moriah encouraging me "to get this book written." And a year later, for better or worse, here it is.

I gratefully acknowledge all of the widows I have had the privilege to know over the years, beginning with Mattie Young, who have prayed and will continue to pray for the church to be the pure and undefiled bride that God desires her to be. And a special remembrance for all those widows who are now in the presence of Jesus: Martha Adkins, Phyllis Anderson, Evangelist Lois Arnold, Edna Beasley, Margaret Bedwell, Edith Bell, Inez Bishop, Marion Bolin, Rosa Lee Bonds, Ruth Ellen Brookes, Louise Burke, Gay Carter, Margaret Cooley, Emma Davenport, Gerda David, Ruth Downing, Geneva Edmond, Eula Ellison, Ginny Gamble, Gertrude Gaston, Bessie Grayson, Odessa Green, Katherine Guinn, Dolly Hayes, Lee Henson, Norrine Hickman, Clemmie Holmes, Mary Hunnicut, Helen Israel, Isabel Jones, Wanda

Sue Jones, Sylvia Kendricks, Mickey Kenemer, Paralee McWilliams, Ruth Mitchell, Annie Moore, Isabel Morris, Chris Morrow, Nancy Morrow, Gloria Nabors, Nancy Oliver, Dollie Potts, Nancy Ransom, Willene Reynolds, Lorene Richardson, Lorrine Robbs, Gladys Seitz, Irene Stinson, Evangelist Agnes Stokes, Carolyn Stutsman, Camille Stubbs, Dorothy Swinson, Bertha Tolliver, Dorothy Turner, Willa Turner, Beulah Mae Vasser, Elvenia Walker, Pearl Watkins, Gracy Mae Woods, Essie Williams, and Mattie Young, the widow whom God used to start Widows Harvest Ministries.

And finally, I thank all of those who have faithfully prayed for Widows Harvest Ministries as well as supported it financially for almost thirty years now. There are no words to express my feelings for each of these people. It would be impossible to name all of them here, but they know who they are. And more importantly, God does.

* * *

* * *

Front Cover Photo by Asher Love (Mendonsa), Cover Design by Andy Mendonsa, and Cover Layout by Christopher Johnston

Author Photo, Self-Portrait by Andy Mendonsa, "For now we see in a mirror dimly" (NASB).

Dedication Page Photo by Asher Love (Mendonsa), taken of he and his sister for Gloria, their mother, as a Mother's Day gift, May 2005.

Introduction

According to Genesis 2:15, after God created Adam and placed him in the Garden of Eden, Adam's purpose was to worship God with all his being through "dressing and keeping the garden." That same purpose, figuratively, for all who are in Jesus is, in effect, restated by Jesus in John 4:23, during his encounter with the Samaritan woman at the well when he tells her that his Father desires his "true worshippers to worship him in spirit and in truth, for they are the kind of worshipers the Father seeks" (NIV).

It therefore becomes essential that we accurately define worship in order to understand more fully what Jesus meant by "worship in spirit and in truth," so that we will then be able to gauge for ourselves the degree to which we might have been seduced by the subtleties of deception that Paul warns us about in 2 Corinthians 11:3: "But I am afraid that, as the serpent deceived Eve by his craftiness, your minds will be led astray from the simplicity and purity of devotion to Christ." (NASB)

And just as Eve was deceived first, before becoming the deceiver of Adam, so we have likewise struggled with deception, both individually and corporately, for over two thousand years. And with every deception, we will potentially become the deceived. And once deceived, we will then become the deceiver of others: deception → deceived → deceiver.

How then are we to determine not only whether deception has entered into the church but also, even worse, if we have been deceived and have now become the deceivers of others? The most accurate means for determining our deception must always, I have come to believe, begin with the way we define worship, because that definition will help us determine what we consider to be the most important components of worship that God desires from us, which will thereafter drive our practices.

After Adam and Eve sinned, committing an act of self-worship by eating fruit only meant for God, which act was considered by God to be an act of idolatry/adultery, they were expelled from the garden. Their newfound condition, that of having been separated from God, then became one of *spiritual widowhood*, which is also our own condition when we are apart from Jesus.

Consequently, when we do not understand our condition of *spiritual widowhood* apart from Jesus, (1) we will not fully recognize what Jesus has done for us; (2) we will not fully understand the way that God sees and relates to us; (3) we will not understand why we are vulnerable to being deceived as Eve was deceived by the Serpent; and (4) we will not understand what an accurate assessment of our own condition of being "as a pure virgin" is based on (2 Corinthians 11:1–3, NIV).

Therefore, our not understanding these four points will mean, in all likelihood, that we will have no concern for the plight of those who are physically widowed and fatherless (James 1:27); and if we do not care for those such as these, then we probably do not have a scripturally based understanding of what it means to worship God in spirit and in truth. And finally, not understanding any of these points makes it unlikely that we will know when, as stated in Matthew 24:15 and Mark 13:14, the "abomination of desolation [is] standing where it should not" (and the only place it should not stand is in the church).

Almost thirty years ago, after I read James 1:27 for the first time, this one verse became the key passage of scripture that began to open the door for me to expand my understanding for what defines worship, especially outside the context of a worship service. And based on that understanding, I have ultimately been led to understand our own condition of *spiritual widowhood* apart from Jesus, why this is so, and how to accurately assess the condition of the church based on this understanding.

Understanding worship, then, becomes all-essential, because it is our understanding of worship, and the shape of our subsequent worship practices, that affects the overall health and well-being of the church more than any other single factor.

Every few years a new movement seems to sweep the church in the United States. This usually happens when a book is published and is perceived as being "the answer" for mobilizing the church. Sometimes this book is based on a pastor's success with his own church. In such a case, what is perceived as having caused that success suddenly becomes the blueprint for every other church so that they may achieve the same results. This phenomenon reminds me of what Paul says to the church in Ephesus in Ephesians 4:14: "Then we will no longer be infants, tossed back and forth by the waves, and blown here and there by every wind of teaching and by the cunning and craftiness of people in their deceitful scheming" (NIV).

If a car engine has a broken crankshaft or has thrown a rod, a tune-up will not fix it or even cause it to run better. That's what all of these movements might be likened to: trying to tune up our churches as a solution for something far more serious than worn-out spark plugs. These movements, and all of us have seen them come and go, will never make us into the church that God desires us to be because they are based on a wrong diagnosis. They assume that what we have come to know and accept as the accurate way of fundamental operation for our churches is scripturally correct. Therefore, all we need to do is tweak the churches a little, give them a good tune-up, and then they should run the way God intends for them to. It is not that these movements are wrong or that they are not scripturally sound. The problem lies in the fact that churches are not in need of a tune-up but an entire engine overhaul. This is something that the Jewish leaders in Israel were never willing to do, even when Jesus confronted them with the need for it, and is it likely something that present-day churches will not be willing to do, either, or even to consider for that matter

Much like taking a car with engine trouble into a shop and having it diagnosed by a mechanic and/or a diagnostic machine, the purpose of *Spiritual Widowhood* is ultimately to provide a diagnosis of the present-day church by comparing it with what is written in the Bible in order to determine an accurate diagnosis. It will only be when we know what the root cause of the problem or condition is and then become willing to correct it that any sort of a tune-up might be warranted to make us more effective going forward.

All that follows is what I have now come to refer to as Widow, Bride, and Marriage Theology, which began to take shape as a result of an expanded understanding of James 1:27. Therefore, the majority of *Spiritual Widowhood* focuses on this one passage in James, especially in the context of worship. And it is my hope for anyone who might take the time to read *Spiritual Widowhood* that it will become clear why it is so important for us, as the betrothed of Jesus, to understand all of scripture in the context of our relationship with him from a Widow, Bride and Marriage theological perspective, so, that we might be, as Paul says in 2 Corinthians 11:2, "presented as a pure virgin to Christ", lest we become, as Paul expresses his fears for us in the very next verse, "…that just as Eve was deceived by the serpent's cunning, our minds may somehow be led astray from our sincere and pure devotion to Christ." (NIV).

Chapter 1: Who Is a Widow?

If Jeff Foxworthy said in one of his comedy routines, "You might be a widow if…," his choice of answers would need to include more than *Merriam-Webster's* definition of *widow*. Also, there wouldn't be a punch line, because there is nothing humorous about widowhood.

When I first started Widows Harvest Ministries (WHM), the definition of a widow that seemed to be most commonly accepted for qualifying a woman who had lost her husband to receive help was that found in 1 Timothy 5:9–10:

> No widow may be put on the list of widows unless she is over sixty, has been faithful to her husband, and is well known for her good deeds, such as bringing up children, showing hospitality, washing the feet of the Lord's people, helping those in trouble and devoting herself to all kinds of good deeds (NIV).

Prior to starting WHM (originally called the Chattanooga Widows Ministry), I had been working for a ministry in an inner-city neighborhood in Chattanooga, appropriately named Inner City Ministries (ICM). At that time, it was located on Mitchell Avenue in a building that had previously been a YMCA. Known both as the Old South Side YMCA and the Industrial Y. This building was built in 1929 in the Spanish-mission-style design common to this era, with stucco exterior walls and terra-cotta-tile roof. Back in Chattanooga's industrial heyday, men from rural areas (both from Tennessee and surrounding states like Georgia and Alabama) would stay here while looking for jobs in one of the many local industries, thus the name the Industrial Y. It was also occasionally referred to as the Pink Y, a nickname it earned because the exterior stucco had been repainted a pale pinkish color.

I had also been told that sometime around the early part of the twentieth century, the neighborhood where ICM was located had been home to both Greek and Italian immigrants. Over the years, I would have this confirmed to me by several Greek and Italian descendants I met who were still living in Chattanooga and whose parents or grandparents had first lived in this neighborhood. The greatest evidence for this, though, was a little Italian widow who was still living in the neighborhood when I first started working there. Her English, still very broken, but she could speak just enough to ask for help from time to time with things on her home that needed immediate attention and couldn't wait for one of her sons living across town to come and fix.

One further note: this neighborhood was built on the site of an area that had once been used as a fort during the Civil War. This fort, also known as Fort Phelps, was named for Union Major General James Negley and was used during the Union Army's siege of Chattanooga in 1863. Today, roughly this same area, which now encompasses all of Mitchell Avenue and Reed Avenue, is known as the Fort Negley neighborhood.

By the time I started working in Fort Negley, the residents were a fairly even mix of low-income working-class and non-working-class African Americans, with many of the homes being rental properties owned by slumlords. And the crime rate was one of the highest in the city, with the crimes ranging from prostitution to murder. I would end up spending seventeen years in this neighborhood before I moved my office to my home in another urban neighborhood, St. Elmo, which sits at the foot of Lookout Mountain. Today, however, Fort Negley has undergone a renaissance of sorts, making it almost unrecognizable when compared to the depressed area it was back when I first started serving there. Instead of seeing prostitutes walking the streets, one now observes young white middle-class mothers pushing strollers along the sidewalks. Adding yet another layer of change on the history of this area.

It was while I was working for ICM in this neighborhood that God first began to call my attention to the home-repair needs of older low-income African American widows living in the area. And after seeking God through prayer for almost a year, I finally felt the time had arrived for me to resign from my position at ICM and start a ministry to widows, a ministry that would have as its mission: *Pleading the case of widows* (Isaiah 1:17), *Providing assistance to widows* (primarily home repair; see James 1:27), *and Promoting the spiritual growth and ministries of widows* (primarily prayer; see 1 Timothy 5:5 and the example of Anna the prophetess in Luke 2).

As mentioned previously, what church leaders most commonly defined a widow by and the criteria used to determine her qualifications for help was I Timothy 5:9-10. In my heart, I did not feel that this was an accurate interpretation, though. Many, if not most, of the widows I had been helping certainly did not qualify based on these verses in 1 Timothy 5, but who was I to question this interpretation of scripture? After all, I didn't have a seminary degree. The only degree I had was the bachelor's in journalism with a focus on filmmaking I'd earned from the University of Georgia. But even if my gut instincts were right, I was severely lacking in both knowledge and credibility.

I can't remember whether it was the same year that I started WHM or the next year (1988), but it was while I was driving in my car with the radio tuned to the local Moody broadcast station (WMBW) that I heard a Bible study by John MacArthur being aired on the topic of *"Caring for Widows."* And it would be through MacArthur's teaching on this subject, taken from 1 Timothy 5, that I first learned from both a credible and scholarly source the type of person we should consider to be a scripturally defined widow qualifying for help.

MacArthur, in this series, points out that the Greek word for *widow* in the New Testament is *chēra*, which means "bereft." "That it is, quite literally, the condition of a woman being 'bereft' of a husband that scripturally qualifies her for being helped, and not the circumstance that caused this condition, i.e. divorce, abandonment, death, imprisonment,

3

in a nursing home, or completely disabled (physically, mentally or both)."[1]

Additionally, according to *Strong's Concordance*, this same Greek word for *widow* also means "metaphorically—a city stripped of its inhabitants and riches is represented under the figure of a widow, a presumed derivative whose root base presents the idea of deficiency; a widow (as lacking a husband), literally or figuratively:—widow."[2] Similarly, in the Old Testament, "the Hebrew word for *widow*[,] *'almanah*, conveys similar meaning. *'Almanah* is translated as the word *widow* 53 times, and desolate place and desolate house (palace) 1 time each."[3]

Interestingly, in my trying to understand who should be considered a widow according to the scriptural definition, MacArthur's Bible study "*Caring for Widows*" not only brought clarity to those once muddied waters but also provided an explanation for the widow's qualifications listed in 1 Timothy 5:9–10. Essentially, the purpose of this list was to make clear which people were to be recognized as widows qualified to serve in an official capacity in the church: the "office of widow," if you will.[4]

This office certainly makes sense when you think about the instruction in Titus 2:3–5 for the older women to teach the younger women. Unfortunately, even though the idea that older women should teach younger women is often preached, taught, and endorsed in many churches, making actual provision for this to be carried out in an official capacity almost never seems to occur. Given the fact that scripture prescribes that the older women teach the younger women, you would think that separate but equal systems would be implemented to carry out this instruction by putting the task directly under the oversight of those widows who qualify to serve in the "office of widow." The very idea, though, that there might actually be an officially recognized office for a woman seems to scare most church leaders as much as, if not more than, the Devil himself does.

Suffice it to say that even if no one among a church's leadership is willing to allow an official "office of widow" to be recognized and its duties to be carried out in their congregations, surely it could be an unofficially recognized office. And older widows could still be enlisted to teach, counsel, and disciple younger women. Simply stated, if conscience will not allow ordination of women to the office of widow, then simply don't ordain them, but literally for the sake of the kingdom ("thy kingdom come"), recognize widows and enlist them to serve. Based on the thousands of widows I have been privileged to know over the years, I do not think that most older widows would care whether they were ordained or not. They just want to be recognized for their calling and have provisions made for them to serve.

Chapter 2: Israel a Widow

Even with the interpretation based on John McArthur's view regarding what scripturally defines a widow, i.e., "the condition of being bereft of a husband and not the circumstance that caused it," there may be some who still understandably have doubts, especially given the fact that I have never found anyone who has graduated from seminary who can recall having a class that covered the subject of widows, how they should be scripturally defined, the necessity for their care, or what kingdom role(s) they have been called to fulfill.

Perhaps looking at the nation of Israel and the way that Isaiah identifies Israel as having been a widow will give credence to MacArthur's broader scriptural definition of a widow. Isaiah 54:4 reads, "Do not be afraid; you will not be put to shame. Do not fear disgrace; you will not be humiliated. You will forget the shame of your youth and remember no more the reproach of your widowhood"(NIV). We know that Israel's husband was God and that he didn't die, which means that the "widowhood" spoken of in this passage has to be for a circumstance other than death.

So, if any doubts remain that a woman should be considered a widow if she loses her husband in any way other than through death, all we have to do is look at Israel and the basis for her condition of widowhood. Jeremiah 3:8 reads, "And I saw, when for all the causes whereby backsliding Israel committed adultery I had put her away, and given her a bill of divorce; yet her treacherous sister Judah feared not, but went and played the harlot also"(KJV). In our relationship with God, idolatry and adultery are synonymous.

Neither with Adam and Eve, nor with Israel beginning with God's covenant with Abraham, do we seem to place much significance on their having been in a marriage relationship with God. This, perhaps, may be one of Satan's greatest feats of deception in modern church history. Hopefully by the end of *Spiritual Widowhood*, readers will have gained more insight into the how and why regarding this deception's having overtaken us. Remember that once we are deceived, we are highly prone, and more likely than not, to become the deceivers.

Chapter 3: Biblical Precedent and the Precedent for Adultery as Grounds for Divorce

I
f you have ever seen a court trial on TV or read about one in a book, then you are probably familiar with the term *legal precedent*. Often when one attorney makes an objection to what the opposing attorney is trying to introduce as evidence, he or she will cite a decision made in a previous court case as the grounds for his or her objection. It is then up to the presiding judge to make the determination as to whether the previous court decision applies to his or her objection. The *Free Dictionary* defines *precedent* as "(a) an act or instance that may be used as an example in dealing with subsequent similar instances, and (b) law, a judicial decision that is binding on other equal lower courts in the same jurisdiction as to its conclusion on a point of law, and may also be persuasive to courts in other jurisdictions, in subsequent cases involving sufficiently similar facts."[5]

You may not have thought about this, but every time we quote the Bible to someone, especially for the purpose of correction, we are essentially citing what I have come to think of as biblical precedent. To take that one step further, I have also come to believe that the entirety of scripture is based on the precedents that were, majorly, first set in the Garden of Eden through the fall and exile of Adam and Eve. For instance, Jesus could not be the "last Adam" (1 Corinthians 15:45) if there had not been a first Adam. Another example would be Jesus's "high priesthood after the order of Melchisedec." (Hebrews 5:10 KJV).

So my question became, what is the biblical precedent, then, for adultery to be the grounds for divorce? Adultery was the grounds given for God's divorcing Israel in Jeremiah 3:8. Following are Jesus's own words in Matthew 19:9: "I tell you that anyone who divorces his wife, except for sexual immorality, and marries another woman commits adultery" (NIV).

I have come to believe the answer to this question of biblical precedent to be of such critical importance going forward because it continues to be an area of such great deception (and the history of Israel bears this out) resulting in the devastating consequences for those betrothed to Jesus. If we do not understand the basis for what defines a widow and why a widow is so defined, then we will not understand our own condition of *spiritual widowhood* apart from Jesus and, therefore, why it is of such critical importance that we both honor and provide those physically widowed with care.

Chapter 4: A Promise in the Garden

Quite a few years ago I wrote a booklet called *A Promise in the Garden*. What prompted me to write this book was something that struck me one day while reading 1 Corinthians 11:1–4, which reads as follows:

> I hope you would put up with me in a little foolishness. Yes, please put up with me! I am jealous for you with a godly jealousy. I promised you to one husband, to Christ, so that I might present you as a pure virgin to him. But I am afraid that just as Eve was deceived by the serpent's cunning, your minds may somehow be led astray from your sincere and pure devotion to Christ. For if someone comes to you and preaches a Jesus other than the Jesus we preached, or if you received a different spirit from the Spirit you received, or a different gospel from the one you accepted, you put up with it easily enough (NIV).

What I had never understood about this passage was the simple yet profound fact that Paul, in addressing the church, is speaking to both men and women—not just women. When he expresses his concern that "the church," that is, Christ's bride, not be deceived as Eve was by the Serpent, he is speaking to men and women, because "the church" includes both. Yet historically it has been men who have been the appointed leaders of churches. And just as it was Adam's responsibility not to allow deception to come into the garden, so it has been the same for men throughout the church age. If you do not recognize your own vulnerability as a man, and thus the vulnerability of the church, for being deceived as Eve was by the Serpent, then chances are you have already been deceived and may have now become a deceiver of others.

As a man, once I surrendered my life and became a follower of Jesus, anything having to do with Eve I immediately thought applied only to women. Why? Because that is all I had ever heard, read, or been taught. The idea that I, as a man, would have any part in the vulnerability of Eve being deceived was incomprehensible to me. In fact, it influenced my thinking so much that, whether I consciously acknowledged it or not, my attitudes and behavior were far more like those of bridegroom than of bride in my relationship with Jesus. In other words, regarding the great wedding feast for the marriage of the Lamb that we are all anticipating, my own deception had blinded me to the reality that I would be on the bride's side of the wedding altar, not the groom's.

Yet for some reason, and I think I know what that reason was, I finally saw and understood myself in the context of the church, that is, as a bride. I understood that for those in Christ, who scripture tells us is the "last and final Adam," the only other role there is for us in this relationship is that of figuratively being, if you will, the last Eve. Or to put it another way, once we accept Jesus, the last Adam, we are no longer identified with the first Adam in any way. God the Father now only sees us as his own children who are betrothed to his son. We are a bride who still struggles in the flesh with sin and whose vulnerability is now that of Eve for being deceived. This insight is what led me to write *A Promise in the Garden*.

Once I began to grasp the idea of being seen by God as the bride of Christ, it began to give rise to the supposition that if we are, as the church, in effect, at least figuratively, if not literally, like the last Eve, then it should be possible to find correlations in scripture between the creation of the first Eve through the first Adam and the redemption of the last Eve through the last Adam (i.e., Jesus). In other words, what

I was seeking to satisfy, at least for myself, was the notion that what Jesus ultimately came to do was to redeem a bride, thus making what we believe to be the gospel, literally, a proposal of marriage.

Then my thoughts led me to the place of wondering whether this was scripturally provable. Being the obsessively compulsive person that I am, I set out to prove it. As a result, I do believe that I was able to prove, at least to my satisfaction, that Jesus did indeed come to redeem for himself a bride. And at the time, the greatest evidence that I could find was in the fact that for each one of the verses that describes the creation of Eve through Adam in Genesis 2:21–14, I found a correlating verse (or correlating verses) in the New Testament relating to Jesus in the Gospel accounts, which more than confirmed to me the answer I sought for my original supposition: that we are, in fact, as the church, likened to a "last Eve."

Since writing out the correlations that I found between the creation of the first Eve through Adam, and Jesus coming to redeem a bride, I have been able to arrive at the same conclusion, but from a completely different approach, one that first required an understanding of what scripturally defines a widow. Then, once that had been established, I had to determine who should be considered the first widow—or, if you will, who best exemplified the condition of widowhood—in the Bible.

Chapter 5: The Precedent for Widowhood

Whenever I am asked to share about Widows Harvest with any group interested in learning more about this ministry and ways they might be able to volunteer with us, I will almost always ask the question, "Who was the first widow in the Bible?" Before anyone can answer, though, I will quickly add that this is a trick question. What follows is generally a period of uncomfortable silence before a few cautious answers are given, with the most common one being Ruth, or both Ruth and Naomi.

Before too much time goes by, when I see that no one is probably going to get the right answer, I will remind the group that this is a trick question. Then, someone will usually say, "Eve," and I will quickly follow up with, "Why Eve?" Finally, in most instances, someone will reluctantly answer as a question, "Adam and Eve?" And again I will ask, "Why?"

Sometimes the person who answers "Adam and Eve" will be able to correctly say why it is both of them, but it is usually with an understanding of only part of what makes them the first *condition* of widowhood.

The answer is that Adam and Eve were considered to be one flesh in God's eyes. Which continues to be God's view of any husband and wife today. Adam and Eve are also the biblical precedent for God's view of marriage. Also true is the fact that God considers us to be one with Jesus as his betrothed/bride, which also means, according to Jewish tradition, that God considers us to be already married to Jesus. If this were not the case then why would Joseph contemplate divorcing Mary after he learns that she is pregnant (Mat 1:19)? If they had not already been considered married before the marriage ceremony took place, then the requirement to divorce her would not have been necessary.

That is why when God sees us now, betrothed to Jesus, we are identified only with Jesus and never again with the first Adam. Thus, God extends his never-ending grace to us for our vulnerability for being deceived as Eve was. The proof, perhaps, still remains to be seen, though, for what makes Adam and Eve as "one," the first condition of widowhood in the Bible.

Chapter 6: "So He Drove Out"

Many of the people with whom I have shared these same understandings of scripture with over the years are almost always surprised to find out why Adam and Eve represent the first condition of widowhood in the Bible. Yet these same people almost always seem quick to begin to grasp its significance, namely, the way it relates to their own relationship with Jesus, first as *spiritual widow* and then as *redeemed bride*.

After Eve was deceived by the Serpent and became the deceiver of Adam, God exiled them both from the Garden of Eden. Genesis 3:24 reads, "So he drove out the man; and placed at the east of the garden of Eden cherubims, and a flaming sword which turned every way, to keep the way of the tree of life" (KJV).

What I spoke of in this chapter's first paragraph as being a surprise to most people is the proof that I have presented for Adam and Eve representing the first condition of widowhood, and that proof is the Hebrew verb, *garish*, translated in this passage as "drove out." Of the forty-seven times this word appears in the Old Testament, two times the word is translated as "divorced," and in a third instance it is translated as "a divorced woman."[6] And even though when God speaks of "putting Israel away and giving her a certificate of divorce for her adultery" in Jeremiah 3:8, and "certificate of divorce," a noun, has not been translated from the word, *garish*, a verb, God's reason is the same, with the same action being taken by Him. The consequences of the Israelites' sin caused them to become "bereft of their husband." Not only did their physical reality become a place of desolation, but also their spiritual reality became that which now determines the physical condition of widowhood, namely, "desolate/bereft of a husband."

Like Adam and Eve, the Israelites' sin of adultery, given their "treacherous sister Judah who also played the harlot," was essentially the same. The only command given to Adam by God was that "he could eat fruit from any tree in the garden except the tree of knowledge of good and evil" (Genesis 2:16–17). Prior to both Adam and Eve eating of this fruit that was clearly only meant for God, they had no self-awareness. All of their thoughts and actions were "pure and undefiled."

Only after Adam ate the fruit too did both he and Eve realize, for the first time, that they were naked, so they tried to hide their shame from God. Adam and Eve, in essence, ate fruit that was meant only for God, thereby committing the sinful act of self-worship. For them to worship anything or anyone other than God was an act of both adultery and idolatry. First with Israel in her relationship with God, and then repeated by Christ's bride, the church, throughout the church age, adultery and idolatry remain synonymous. The consequences for sin stemming from acts of impure and defiled worship gone unchecked has had, and will always have, the same outcome: desolation.

However, God did not completely abandon Adam and Eve after he divorced them. He instead chose to pursue them as a bridegroom would pursue a prospective bride by promising the Serpent in Genesis 3:15, "I will put enmity between thee and the woman, and between thy seed and her seed; it shall bruise thy head, and thou shalt bruise his heel" (KJV).

The one who fulfills this promise made to the Serpent is, we as Christ's betrothed believe, Jesus, God's own Son, whom the former sent to be Lord and Savior, as well as Bridegroom, in offering up his life for us. And this one promise was actually the threefold promise for *deliverance, redemption, and restoration.* Jesus became the only way for us to gain entry back into the paradise that was blocked after Adam and Eve were driven out and that remains guarded.

All though, Jesus as Bridegroom is far away from how we relate to him, it may be the most relationally significant one for us to understand.

Apart from Jesus, we are literally *spiritually widowed and fatherless.* In effect, Jesus came to redeem a bride, which essentially makes what we consider to be the gospel a proposal of marriage. So when we accept Jesus's proposal of marriage, we are not only considered to be instantly married but are also, at the same time, instantly adopted into our heavenly Father's family as his children, thus becoming coheirs with Christ.

Thus, Jesus is the fulfillment of the promise that gives us hope for *deliverance, redemption, and restoration,* beginning with his proposal of marriage and our acceptance, making us his bride who remains faithfully betrothed to him until the day of the great wedding feast and the marriage of the Lamb, after which we will remain with him for all eternity in the place that he has prepared for us in his Father's house.

Chapter 7: Introducing James 1:27

Unlike the way I have begun *Spiritual Widowhood*, typically, when speaking to a group for the first time about Widows Harvest Ministries (WHM), I begin by quoting James 1:27, the scripture this ministry was founded on. I will then begin to break down this passage almost word by word and line by line in order to present what has been for the most part overlooked in order to discover its overall significance and far-reaching implications for us as Jesus's betrothed. In fact, I have now come to refer to this passage as the *"bride passage."* It presents Jesus's instructions to his bride for her need to remain "chaste as a virgin."

The reason, though, I decided not to approach *Spiritual Widowhood* in the way I typically do when addressing a group about WHM is because of a young mother and wife, Moriah Bond, who had been in a couples' small group when I recently taught a Bible study on Widow, Bride, and Marriage Theology, suggested I take a different tack. She wrote me a letter several months after this study was over and told me she had awakened in the middle of the night about half-way thru this study and in her own words wrote *"I felt CERTAIN the Lord was telling me you've got to get this book written. So here's your confirmation if you ever felt like you were supposed to get this book written."* Additionally, based on the Bible study material I used to teach the small group she was a part of, she suggested an order of content for me to follow. To that end I have taken her advice and started this book by first establishing our spiritual condition for being *spiritually widowed* apart from Jesus as the consequence of the fall.

It was amazing how obvious it became to me that the order of content Moriah suggested in her letter would be a much more effective way of approaching *Spiritual Widowhood* given what I have come to understand as a greatly expanded interpretation of James 1:27. And by *expanded*, what I mean is that it isn't found in commentaries. Nor is it, for the most part, the generally accepted academic interpretation. Whether I am successful in being able to do this will ultimately be determined by how clearly I am able to present this in written form as opposed to speaking it. As for outcomes based on what is taken away from *Spiritual Widowhood*, thankfully I am only responsible for delivering a message the best I am able to. This message, however, is one that I feel has been more than confirmed to me over the years through the outcomes I have personally seen and experienced as a result of the widows ministry that God called me to beginning in the spring of 1986.

Before actually diving into James 1:27, I wish to discuss why I refer to it as the "bride passage": because this single little three-line passage actually sums up the Fall of humankind, our resulting spiritual condition of being widowed and orphaned, and God's promise to send a Savior, who will also be our bridegroom and husband, to *deliver, redeem, and restore* us. As long as we remain in this world, James 1:27 provides us with a litmus test, if you will, for being able to determine whether we are fulfilling his desire for us to remain "a chaste virgin" and not be deceived as Eve was by the Serpent.

Chapter 8: "Religion"

The first line of James 1:27 states that "pure and undefiled religion before our father is this." Some translations put a colon after the word *this*, but several use a comma. Either way, what follows the punctuation mark appears to be a list of two separate conditions for a "pure and undefiled religion" if the religion is to be accepted by God. The first one, "visiting the widows and the fatherless," seems to be pretty straightforward, but the condition that begins with "and" and is followed by "to keep oneself unpolluted by the world" is somewhat ambiguous and, at the very least, highly subjective. This doesn't make a great deal of sense to me; it is something I struggled with for quite a number of years. The conclusion that I have finally arrived at for this last line, though, won't be discussed at length until chapter 23. The rest of this chapter will focus solely on the word *religion*, found in the first line of James 1:27.

I first read James 1:27 during a time when I was searching God for an answer to the question, is there a need to start a ministry to widows? I instantly knew, based on this passage, that the answer was an emphatic yes. In the weeks and months that followed that realization, as I sought an answer from God for the second question—should I be the one to start a ministry to widows?—what really continued to drive me, as more and more widows began to contact me with home-repair needs, was the phrase *pure and undefiled*. The two words *pure* and *undefiled*, in my mind, were describing characteristics that could be attributed to no one but Jesus. And in the context of the act of "visiting widows and the fatherless in their distress," these acts could be characterized as nothing less than Christlikeness.

It was the word *religion* that I really struggled with, though. I did not understand at all why this word was being used here. Since becoming a follower of Jesus, I found that the word *religion* had very negative connotations. Being religious was akin to thinking that you were a pretty good person because of the way you viewed yourself for the ways you treated others and for supporting what you considered to be good causes. In essence, religious people based their hope of going to heaven on their good works and did not consider that they might be going to heaven because they accepted Jesus's proposal of marriage and had been subsequently adopted into God's family.

My struggles with the word *religion* would continue to plague me for several years. And it would not be until I had the Bible reference resources (this was before computers were available) to be able to look up the meaning of the original Greek word translated as "religion" in this passage that I was finally able to understand the actual intent of the word's meaning.

I probably shouldn't have been, but I was nonetheless surprised to learn that the word *religion*, from the Greek word *threskeia*,[7] essentially means "worship." The more I thought about it, though, the more sense it made. After all, isn't worship the expression of our stated beliefs through our words, deeds, and actions offered up to God, especially in fulfilling what it means to love God with all of our heart, mind, and soul, and to love our neighbor as ourselves?

Prior to this discovery, I had always defined worship by a worship service and what generally takes place during that time: singing, taking up an offering, reading scripture, praying, and preaching. Unless all of the widows and fatherless in their distress show up on Sunday morning for the worship service, James 1:27 is instructing us, Jesus's bride, to go beyond a worship service, beyond the church walls, in order to fulfill what God considers to be "pure and undefiled worship."

Since I had never heard worship defined in this way but had only heard it used in the context of a worship service, it would take me a number of years to get my head around this new understanding. Yet once I did, I began to realize the serious implications for us as followers of Jesus if we do not understand worship in this way and comprehend what the consequences are for not doing as instructed. Essentially, God views and accepts our worship as being either pure and undefiled or impure and defiled. Inevitably, a critical mass will be reached for one of these, with the former resulting in restoration and with the latter resulting in desolation (i.e. becoming like the widow).

Chapter 9: Worship

As I indicated in chapter 8, it was really hard for me to get my head around the idea of what worship was apart from a worship service. Once I did, though, I began to obsessively pursue trying to get a handle on what I came to see and understand as the differences between a worship-service-centered faith and a worship-through-service-centered faith. This led me to begin making the distinction between a church worship service and the much larger idea of what God intends us to understand and carry out as worship beyond the church walls. That 99.99999 percent of all that God considers to be worship happens outside the church, where each of us is called to "bear Christ's reproach" through acts and offerings of worship (Hebrews 13:13–14).

What led me to this understanding during my initial search for a more accurate definition of worship was the fact that I could not actually find any New Testament passages that specifically called believers gathering together like we do today a worship service. The book that was of particular interest to me in this search was 1 Corinthians. The members of the church at Corinth were doing so much wrong that Paul's letters to them seemed to be equally for the purpose of instruction as they were for the purpose of correction. And as a result, we are given the only real glimpse into the way an early New Testament church functioned.

Surely, I thought, since Paul was actually giving instructions specifically for what the Corinthians should be doing when they came together, he would use the word *worship* to describe it. Much to my amazement, though, he didn't. In fact, the word *worship* appears only once when Paul is writing to the Corinthians. And even in that one instance, 1 Corinthians 14:25, Paul does not characterize their gathering specifically as worship or a worship service.

Instead, in this single instance the word *worship* is translated from the most commonly used Greek word for worship in the New Testament, *proskyneō*.[8] There are in fact, however, five Greek verbs (including the one just mentioned) and three Greek nouns in the New Testament that have all been translated simply as the verb *worship*, in one tense or the other. In this instance, the word *proskyneō* (which, incidentally, is where we get the word *prostrate*) used here is describing worship in the context of salvation and being demonstrated by the act of falling on one's face, symbolizing a surrendered life.

Then, once we get back up on our feet and begin our new lives as citizens of heaven, all of life brings with it opportunities for us to worship God through the giving of thanks to him in all things (Ephesians 5:20) and through our good works (deed offerings). Ephesians 2:10 reads, "For we are his workmanship, created in Christ Jesus unto good works, which God hath before ordained that we should walk in them."

Just as my study of James 1:27 has spanned more than twenty-five years, my desire to more fully understand what God considers to be worship has led me to try to put into words my own definition of the word. Even after all of the years it has taken for me to attempt the penning of such a definition, almost as soon as I wrote it down I began to contemplate its flaws. Here it is nonetheless. Hopefully through what is presented as part of the remainder of *Spiritual Widowhood*, this definition, as flawed as it may be, will make more sense than it might upon first reading.

Worship is everything that we say and do, everywhere and at all times, in the denial of self, as offerings through our sacrifices, deeds, and works unto the Lord, that fulfills what it means to love the Lord our God with our hearts, minds, and souls, and to love our neighbors as ourselves, especially that which we do outside the camp as we bear Christ's reproach.

Chapter 10: The Precedent for Worship

There is a clear biblical precedent for worship, but it may not be obvious to us today because of the ways in which we have come to define worship, more so that we have a practiced definition and less so that we have a clearly prescribed scriptural definition. As was discussed in chapter 3, a biblical precedent can generally be found for what we would consider to be foundational beliefs and practices of the Christian faith. Worship is not an exception, even though the first time the actual word *worship* appears in the Bible is not until Genesis 22:5, when "Abraham said to his servants, Stay here with the donkey while I and the boy go over there. We will worship, and then we will come back to you" (NIV). The Hebrew word translated as the word *worship* in this case is *shachah*,[9] which has the same basic meaning as the New Testament Greek word for *worship*, which is *proskyneō*. Both words essentially mean "to bow down." In the majority of instances in both the Old Testament and the New Testament where we find the word *worship*, it has been translated from one of these two words.

The first time that worship, not translated as the word *worship*, is described in the Bible is in Genesis 2:15, when we are told that Adam's purpose for being put into the Garden of Eden is "to dress and to keep it." The Hebrew word for *to dress it* is the word *'abad*,[10] which is akin to the Greek New Testament word *latreuo*,[11] both of which mean "to serve" in the context of worship.

Take for instance Romans 12:1: "Therefore I urge you, brethren, by the mercies of God, to present your bodies a living and holy sacrifice, acceptable to God, which is your spiritual service of worship"(NASB). *Latreuo* has been translated in the King James Version as the word *service*, but the New International Version also translates it as the word *worship*. Paul tells us that "by the mercies of God," mercies that we continue to receive throughout our lives, we are to be "living and holy sacrifices" (with Jesus being the first living and holy sacrifice), which God, in turn, considers to be our "spiritual service of worship" (again, with Jesus's life serving as our model).

Hopefully, this is not getting too confusing, but I just wanted to bring out the point that Adam's purpose was to worship God with his whole being, which included the "dressing and keeping of the garden." His worship should also be characterized as being "pure and undefiled" just by virtue of the fact that he was without sin in a setting where sin had never entered.

After the Fall, though, Adam and Eve's once "pure and undefiled" acts of worship became impure and defiled and were no longer a pleasing aroma to God. This meant that acts of worship / good works were insufficient to atone for their act of self-worship or to reverse its consequences. Obviously, if offerings of good works had been sufficient, then God would have let Adam and Eve remain in the garden. That he didn't establishes the precedent for offerings of good works alone being insufficient for us to gain God's favor apart from Jesus's sacrifice of his life for the atonement of our sins. And it is not until Jesus came to offer his life for us as this one-time-atonement for sin that we are given a second picture of "pure and undefiled" acts of worship by a man born without sin, but this time the setting is in a sin-filled world. This picture, or example, has been given to us through all four Gospel accounts that record for us Jesus's own words and also describe many of his deeds and works leading up to his death. Simply put, Jesus modeled for us, as the sinless last Adam, what it means to worship in a fallen and sinful world, a model that stood in stark contrast to the picture of worship that was being modeled by the religious leaders for those whom they served as shepherd. This, I might add, is a dynamic and a tension that still exists today.

It is interesting to note that God gave Adam only one command (Genesis 2:16–17): not to eat from the tree of the knowledge of good and evil (Genesis 2:17). God warned Adam that to eat of this tree would mean death. As long as Adam and Eve remained faithful in carrying out God's stated purpose for them in the garden, they would never experience death. Obviously, when they disobeyed God's one command, they brought death not only upon themselves but also upon all of humankind.

It is very striking to compare the command that God gave to Adam with the new commandment that Jesus gives to us in John 13:34–35: "A new command I give you: Love one another. As I have loved you, so you must love one another. By this everyone will know that you are my disciples, if you love one another" (NIV).

The Fall brought with it the corruption of perfect love. Perfect love has no thought of self but thinks only of others, and most importantly of God. Jesus's new commandment, to love one another, is obviously not new at all but is one that sums up all the other commandments, including the two greatest commandments. Loving others is our single greatest struggle. Jesus has given us the perfect model for what this looks like, and what it looks like on the whole happens to be a perfect picture of worship. Loving one another begins with having a relationship with Jesus, and then following his example for serving and not being served. Perhaps 1 John 4:18 puts it best: "There is no fear in love; but perfect love casts out fear, because fear involves punishment, and the one who fears is not perfected in love" (NASB).

As soon as Adam took a bite of the apple, both he and Eve became aware of their nakedness. And here we know that perfect love has been corrupted, because it is out of fear that they tried to hide from God what they have done—and who can blame them, because the consequences of their sin brought with it unimaginable torment. The same remains true today: there is no hiding anything from God, and our sins will always find us out. This is something that is equally true for us as individuals, as church bodies, and as the church universal. Yet, even knowing that the fear of God is the beginning of wisdom, it would seem, at least today, that we struggle much more with a fear of human beings than a fear of God. It is worth noting that the opposite of wisdom is said to be foolishness. So, in the case of Christians, the fear of humankind would not so much be the beginning of foolishness but more like the perpetuation of it.

Chapter 11: "Undefiled"

O nce I had begun to understand the word *religion* in the context of worship, especially making the connection between the word and the origins of worship tied to God's purpose for Adam in the Garden of Eden, new insights for the significance of "visiting the widows and the fatherless in their distress" as an "undefiled" act of worship began to bring with them greater clarity for me in my own relationship with Jesus as husband/bridegroom.

So, the next word to examine in this study, also in the first line of James 1:27, is *undefiled*, which in the original Greek language is the word *amiantos*, which simply means "not defiled, unsoiled."[12] Ironically, at one point in history, it was also the word used for asbestos, "so called because it showed no mark or stain when thrown into fire"[13]— which is precisely what happened to Shadrach, Meshach, and Abednego when they "were thrown into the fiery furnace"(Daniel 3:22–26).

This word, perhaps more than any other word in James 1:27, is what began to open my eyes to this passage's significance as being what I have come to characterize as the instruction from Jesus as bridegroom to the Church as bride for remaining "pure as a virgin" (NIV) and as such, being perhaps, one of the strongest indicators for our not being deceived as Eve was by the Serpent. This is especially true when considering the fact that the word *undefiled* appears only four times in the New Testament, with each instance being tied directly to a significant aspect of our relationship with Jesus.

The first time that *undefiled* appears is in Hebrews 7:26, in the context of the characterization of Jesus's high priesthood: "For such an high priest became us, who is holy, harmless, *undefiled*, separate from sinners, and made higher than the heavens" (KJV, emphasis added). If this were not so, then Jesus could neither be our High Priest nor be qualified to be our Savior or bridegroom. So, in the first instance where this word is used, it establishes Jesus's high priesthood as being "holy, harmless, [and] undefiled," or to put it simply, he is 100 percent qualified, to the exclusion of all others born of woman on this earth, to be the promised Messiah.

In the second instance when the word *undefiled* is used, it is used quite amazingly in the specific context of marriage. Not surprisingly, perhaps, it is also found in the book of Hebrews. Hebrews 13:4 reads, "Marriage is to be held in honor among all, and the marriage bed is to be *undefiled*: but fornicators and adulterers God will judge" (NASB). Which is exactly what God judged Israel for in Jeremiah 3:8 and why he gave her a "bill of divorce." And because, for so long, I had failed to see and understand our relationship with Jesus as bride, always viewing any passage that spoke of marriage only in the context of physical marriage, I never considered a passage such as this in terms of our marriage relationship to Jesus.

I have realized that if we do not first think of ourselves and the church as being a bride to Jesus and, as such, the most important marriage to always consider first, then we will never be able to truly understand the significance of James 1:27 in this context, or the consequences for our failure to in this regard.

When we do understand *undefiled* in the context of Hebrews 13:4 as pertaining first to both our marriage to Jesus and our worship of our heavenly Father, we become better able to plainly understand and accept that the act of visiting described in James 1:27 literally addresses both what keeps our marriage bed from becoming defiled and what keeps us from being in what God considers to be an adulterous/idolatrous relationship with the world.

Visiting, therefore, becomes one of the most critical acts for us to carry out after we say "I do" in acceptance of Jesus's proposal of marriage. Marriage carries with it responsibilities. For better or for worse, for richer or for poorer, and in sickness and in health, we must honor, obey, love, and cherish our spouse until death do us part. A marriage doesn't work out so well when any of these are not upheld by either the husband or the wife, especially if either one chooses to just lie around the house all day with their feet propped up, watching soap operas and eating bonbons. This is not meant to be sexist, but after all, in our relationship to Jesus, we, both male and female, are considered by God to be his bride. And that is the only reason I use this stereotypical illustration. Each of us could no doubt insert our own list of the ways we feel our spouses have not fulfilled their vow of being faithful.

Although at this point it may still be difficult to understand, much less accept, that Hebrews 13:4 is telling us that we are responsible for obeying Jesus as our spouse if we are to remain undefiled by the world, hopefully further examination of James 1:27 will make plain that this is exactly what the passage is telling us. And essentially a critical component of what we are really asking God to bring about every time we pray the "Lord's Prayer" beseeching him "for thy kingdom come, they will be done, on earth as it is in heaven." Whether we realize it or not, both individually as well as corporately, the more we become the "pure and undefiled bride" that God desires for us to be the greater the indication it is for us that God's kingdom has come and his will is being done on earth as it is in heaven.

Continuing on with this discussion of the word translated as *undefiled*, the third place in the New Testament where this word is used is in James 1:27. Seeing this word only in this passage and not making the connection with *worship* or the other instances where *undefiled* is used, seems to have only had the effect of diminishing the significance of the passage as a whole. Having already looked at two of the four instances when this word has been used, adding this third instance serves only to make it more apparent that the order and contexts in which this word appears could in no way be random or coincidental.

For purposes of reviewing before going on to the fourth instance where the word *undefiled* is used, it is important to remind ourselves that the first time the word *undefiled* is used is to describe Jesus's condition of being sinless and therefore being the only one who is able to atone for our sin. And then, once we accept his proposal of marriage (the gospel), we are betrothed and considered by our heavenly Father to already be married to him. As such, he desires us to "remain chaste as a virgin" (2 Corinthians 11:2), which means keeping the marriage bed undefiled. And then when the word *undefiled* is used in James 1:27, it reveals to us that we are kept from being defiled by the world through acts of "pure and undefiled worship."

Now, keeping all of this in mind, let's look at the fourth and last place where the word *undefiled* is used: in 1 Peter 1:4. Here it is revealed to us what awaits all who are betrothed to Jesus: "to obtain an inheritance which is imperishable and *undefiled*, and will not fade away, reserved in heaven for you" (NASB, emphasis added). Whereas we were once spiritually widowed and God, through Jesus, delivered us from this condition through the redemptive power of Jesus's shed blood, the way has now been made for us to be fully restored to a place like the Garden of Eden (or to the actual Garden of Eden where the way has been blocked), where we will remain with Jesus, as his betrothed, for all eternity.

This word *undefiled* and the four ways it is used in the New Testament, concluding with this last verse in 1 Peter, brings all that we believe our relationship with Jesus to be full circle. Beginning first with the exile of Adam and Eve, we then move on to God's promise to send an undefiled Savior, who will also be bridegroom and husband, to deliver and redeem us so that we might live a faithful life expressed through undefiled acts of worship, all the while living in anticipation of the fully restored life we have been promised in a sinless paradise, where we will receive "an inheritance incorruptible, and undefiled, and that fadeth not away." Or, to put it another way, the idea of being undefiled in the context of not only this verse in James but also of the entirety of scripture, according to Widow, Bride, and Marriage Theology, is this: widowed → delivered, betrothed → redeemed, and finally, married → restored. And all this is evident from just the first sentence of James 1:27.

Chapter 12: "To Visit"

Perhaps the most profound word in James 1:27 is the word *visit*, found in the second line of the passage. First, though, I would like to give you an idea of the span of time that passed between my insights into this passage. It was around 1988 when I first heard John MacArthur's Bible study *"Caring for Widows"* and learned the scripturally based definition of a widow. But it wouldn't be until the year 2000 that I would have a more complete understanding of this passage based on the significance of the infinitive verb *to visit*.

It was during this year that I read Dr. Amy Sherman's newly published devotional *"Sharing God's Heart for the Poor."*[14] Of the seventeen devotions that comprise her book, two of them are devoted to presenting a greatly expanded view of the significance of the infinitive verb *to visit* in James 1:27. Up to that point the only real significance I had attached to this word was in the context of worship. What I mean by this is simply that as I was struggling to understand worship in a larger context (outside of a worship service), one of the points proving to me the idea of visiting was that unless all the widows and the fatherless who are in distress come to a worship service in order for others to minister to them, then worship in this context means that those who would minister have to go visit these individuals where they live. And God considers this to be an act of "pure and undefiled worship."

In her first devotion expounding on the verb *to visit*, Dr. Sherman draws the correlation between "to visit" in James 1:27 and other instances in scripture where God "visits," resulting in the "imparting of life." One example she gives is in 1 Samuel 2:21, where we learn that

Hannah was barren. But after God visits her, she has five children. "The visitation of God imparts life."[15] Another example given is in Luke 7:16, where a widow is mourning the loss of her son, and Jesus, witnessing what is taking place, commands the widow's son to get up, which he does. Those who are witness to this begin to say, "Surely God has visited us!" Thus, the act of visiting in James 1:27 is "the imparting of life."[16]

In her second devotion, Dr. Sherman further connects the verb *to visit* with God's deliverance and redemption of his people, the Jews in the Old Testament. In her first example, she cites Exodus 3:8, when God "comes down to deliver them [the Jews] out of the hand of the Egyptians." Her second example involves Zechariah (in some translations, Zecharias), the father of John the Baptist, when he says in Luke 1:68 (emphasis added), "Blessed be the Lord God of Israel for he hath *visited* and redeemed his people."

I am not a Bible scholar, and I have no claim to be one, but my discovery of these connections that Dr. Sherman makes, tying the word *visit* to both deliverance and redemption, was a very profound insight for me. And it seemed reasonable that if what I had come to understand about worship as mentioned in the first line of James 1:27 was true, then what Dr. Sherman presents about the verb *to visit* appeared to be consistent with this.

John 3:16 reads, "For God so loved the world, that he gave his only begotten son, that whosoever believeth in him should not perish, but have everlasting life" (KJV).

Seeing that God sent his own son *to visit us* in our distress as those who were *spiritually widowed* and in need of *deliverance, redemption, and restoration*, it would stand to reason that what God has mandated for us to fulfill as acts of "pure and undefiled worship by visiting the widow and the fatherless in their distress" should be marked by the life God breathes through such acts—and they should result in the same outcomes mentioned in the Bible. This becomes especially poignant when we begin to understand that the widow and the fatherless not only symbolize for us our own fallen condition but also symbolize what Jesus came to *deliver us from, redeem us for, and restore us to.*

There is an account in the book of Acts, preceding this mandate in James 1:27, that undeniably supports Dr. Sherman's contention that God will breathe life into acts of "visiting the widow and the fatherless in their distress." Found in Acts 1:7, it is the subject of the next chapter.

Chapter 13: Acts 6:7

"The word of God kept on spreading; and the number of disciples continued to increase greatly in Jerusalem, and a great many of the priests were becoming obedient to the faith" (NASB). In effect, what is being described as the outcome here could be characterized as *deliverance and redemption leading to restoration.* It is also the fulfillment of the "great commission" (Matthew 26:19), that is, making disciples.

When you read verse 7, though, without reading or knowing what preceded the results described in Acts 6:1–6, you might think it would stir up the desire in most believers to find out what had caused such extraordinary outcomes. Yet when you read the preceding six verses first, you find that there seems to be somewhat of a disconnect between what took place and the need to discover what was so significant about what had occurred that led to such profound outcomes.

According to most interpretations that I have heard and read over the years for what occurs in Acts 6:1–6, it is almost exclusively thought as being the basis for the creation of the office of deacon, an office that is intended to care for a broad spectrum of needs, including those of widows, but primarily in a church setting. Additionally, in some churches one of the greatest perceived needs for the enlistment of deacons is to free up the pastors so that they might "devote themselves more fully to prayer and the ministry of the word" (Acts 6:4).

Sometimes it seems to me that scripture is interpreted to support how we have come to operate as a church rather than to provide instruction for how a church should operate. What I mean by this is that we look at the way we operate as a church and then we find scriptures that provide the basis for it, as opposed to searching scripture first in order to learn the ways that we should operate as a church. Obviously, if tradition has taught us nothing else, it is that we are quick to assume that what we are doing has been clearly prescribed in scripture. To assume has never been, is never, and will never be a sound approach for us as followers of Jesus.

Unfortunately, I fear it is far too often the case that we, in fact, operate out of an assumed scriptural correctness rather than in a way that questions correctness and goes in search of scriptural certainty. A case in point is one of the main points of *Spiritual Widowhood*, namely, that our definition of worship today is based on assumed scriptural correctness without any scriptural basis for fully supporting said correctness. By virtue of the authority of churches, and in many cases the denominations they are affiliated with, we are far too easily willing to "accept the precepts of men when it comes to doctrinal truth" (Mathew 15:9), or as Paul tells the church in Corinth in 2 Corinthians 11:4, "For if someone comes to you and preaches a Jesus other than the Jesus we preached, or if you received a different spirit from the Spirit you received, or a different gospel from the one you accepted, you put up with it easily enough"(NIV).

What Paul is literally saying here is that we easily accept what we are told is true. And this warning found in the book of 2 Corinthians was written almost two thousand years ago, when the church was in its infancy and had the benefit of firsthand witnesses of the gospel accounts. Imagine how blurred the lines have become for what we easily accept today, which was built on what was likewise easily accepted back then.

I am convinced that the first six verses of Acts 6 is an example of those who have had authority over the church having convinced themselves over time, and then have easily convinced many others over the years, of an interpretation of these verses that completely ignores the true significance about what took place that led to the outcomes reported to us in Acts 6:7. What will therefore be covered in the next four chapters has as its purpose the bringing of more light to bear on what is truly significant about what was actually taking place in Acts 6:1–7 and why. This is also consistent with the *Widow, Bride, and Marriage Theological* perspective of scripture that *Spiritual Widowhood*, as a whole, is intended to present.

Chapter 14: "Desolate"

As indicated at the end of chapter 13, there first needs to be more understanding of the backstory that led up to the critical nature of the need that was identified and responded to in the first six verses of Acts 6 in order to fully understand why the outcomes recorded in Acts 6:7 were so significant.

Keeping this in mind, the first thing we need to include as part of this backstory is several passages of scripture in the gospel accounts relating to widows, or the condition of widowhood, based on Jesus's own words. In Mathew 23:38, Jesus says of the scribes and Pharisees when speaking to the multitudes, "Behold, your house is left unto you desolate" (KJV).

This passage, understandably, might not appear at first as having anything to do with widows, but upon closer examination the word *desolate*, which has been translated from the Greek word *erēmos*, has as one of its meanings "bereft," as in, "of a flock deserted by the shepherd or of a woman neglected by her husband, from who the husband withholds himself."[17]

As was discussed in chapter 1, the New Testament Greek word for *widow* also means "bereft, as in bereft of a husband."[18] Jesus is quite literally saying that Israel has, once again, become like the widow, and that her husband, God, has left the house, so to speak. This is not to mention the fact that Jesus is God, that he is not in a building at the time when he tells this to the scribes and Pharisees, and that they don't even recognize him, which may explain, in part, why the Gospel accounts very seldom record that Jesus even went inside the temple.

The question is, what led to the scribes' and Pharisees' condition as "being a house left desolate?" The answer is revealed, at least in part, when Jesus is in the temple with his disciples toward the end of his ministry. Remembering that Jesus is both man and God, and that humankind judges outward appearances whereas God judges the heart, in Mark 12:38–40 we are given insight into what Jesus's pronouncement in Matthew 23:28 means, as it indicates the outward evidence or symptoms he is basing the heart condition of Israel on. And because this takes place toward the end of Jesus's ministry, it could be interpreted as being a review of what is crucially important for his disciples to remember before they are tested as shepherds of the emerging church after he has been crucified, is resurrected, and ascends into heaven.

Beginning in Mark 12:38, Jesus first warns his disciples to "beware of the scribes" (teachers and interpreters of Jewish law). Then following his initial warning, continuing on through Mark 12:40, he includes as its basis their being dressed in clothing that will bring recognition to them in public, their giving false salutations of love, and finally their taking the chief seats of honor in the synagogues and uppermost rooms at feasts. All of these, of course, are symptoms manifesting themselves outwardly, but they reveal the degree of deception that has overtaken the hearts of the teachers of the law, a deception that has so blinded them that it has caused all of Israel's leaders to be responsible for causing a critical mass of "impure and defiled worship" to be reached. This, in turn, ultimately led to the house they had been entrusted to watch over to become a place of desolation, something that, first, they don't even realize has occurred, and second, they probably wouldn't be willing to take the responsibility for if they did. This is undeniably confirmed by what Jesus reveals next to his disciples. As he continues on with his indictment, a direct connection is made between the condition of the scribes' and Pharisees' hearts, their treatment of widows, and their house being left desolate: "Beware of the scribes … they devour the widow's houses, and for a pretense [for show] make long prayers, these shall receive greater damnation."

If, however, this connection is not completely apparent, by going back to Matthew 23 (often referred to as The Seven Woes to the Scribes and the Pharisees), we find in verse 14 that Jesus has made this same assessment, "Woe unto you, Scribes and Pharisees, hypocrites! For you devour widows' houses, and for a pretense make long prayer: therefore ye shall receive greater damnation" (KJV).

Psalm 68:5 makes it clear that God's character includes being "a father of the fatherless, and a judge of the widows, in his holy habitation" (KJV). As such, it remains critically important for those who would claim Jesus as their betrothed to model God's character in the selfsame way. The warning that Jesus gives to his disciples about the scribes, followed by his basis for it, reveals that having, and even knowing, the truth based on correct interpretations means nothing when it is not lived out. When the only thing we have is what we are told to do, instead of a model that shows us what to do and leads the way for our doing it, the person or corporate entity telling us what to do will always become more the focus of our faith than God is. And as 2 Corinthians 11:4 reveals to us, "We will accept it easily enough."

When we say we are to be imitators of Jesus, which also means being imitators of God our Father, this, perhaps more than anything else, is what lies at the heart of *"pure and undefiled worship."* If we are not this, then our worship is not this, and our house likewise will become like that of the widow: desolate.

To imply that the warning Jesus gave his disciples about the scribes and the basis for its being true is also true for us today might seem unduly harsh. Yet as we continue on in this chapter and look at what Jesus calls his disciples' attention to immediately following his indictment of the scribes, it seems only to add more credence to the plausibility of this prospect.

Verse 41 of Mark 12 reads, "And Jesus sat over against the treasury, and beheld how the people cast money into the treasury: and many that were rich cast in much." What Jesus begins to point out to his disciples is an illustration for them in real time of some of the actual effects of the condition of the scribes' hearts in his indictment against them. He does this first by identifying those with means, and then he contrasts them and their giving with that of a poor widow. Those with means have themselves been deceived, thus becoming equally responsible for "devouring the widows' houses." They have fallen victim to the "yeast of the Pharisees," but they are without excuse (Matthew 16:6). Remember the progression: *deception → deceived → deceiver.*

Immediately following Jesus's observation of the "rich casting in much," he points out the widow at the altar as if to say, "And look at who one of these widows is whose house is being devoured by the scribes. She is not only a widow who exhibits the greatest faith among you by putting into the treasury all she has, but she is also a physical representation for all who are spiritually widowed whom my Father has sent me to *deliver, redeem, and restore.*"

This widow's trust in God is so great that she does not even seem to worry where her next meal will come from. She is all in, so to speak, the evidence clearly being that she puts all she has, monetarily speaking, into the treasury. By contrast, the others whom Jesus has pointed out who are only giving "out of their abundance [surplus]" remain concerned about not only where their next meal will come from but also maintaining their overabundant lifestyles.

Jesus tells us in Luke 12:34, "Where our treasure is so will our hearts also be." When Jesus contrasts the faith of this widow, who gave all she had, with everyone else giving out of their surplus, he is also making the point that a willingness to only give out of the surplus of our personal treasuries is a strong indication that we are only willing to give out of the surplus in all other areas of our lives as pertaining to God's service. And quite profoundly the evidence that most reveals this deception is being exposed at the very altar of the Lord.

So, to put it another way, the evidence for those giving out of their own surplus, having been deceived by the religious leaders, was this widow whose house was being devoured as a consequence of this deception but who, at the same time, had not become deceived in her own faith, which stood in stark contrast to that of the others.

In addition to the passages of the New Testament just covered as part of the backstory needing to be understood, there is one section of scripture in the Old Testament that is particularly relevant to this discussion that is found in Zechariah 7.

In this chapter, through God's prophet Zechariah, God questions if the "observance of the fasts the fifth and seventh months" of the people of Bethel was really done "unto me, even to me." Likewise, he asks in verse 7:6, "When you did eat, and when you did drink, did you eat for yourselves, and drink for yourselves?" Then God goes on to explain why he questions whether the people of Bethel have really been doing these things unto him. In similar fashion to Jesus's indictment of the scribes, God tells the people what he is charging them with in verses 7:9–10, namely, being guilty of not "executing true judgment and showing mercy and compassion, and causing the widow, the fatherless, the stranger and the poor to be oppressed as well as harboring hate against each other."

God then tells the people in verse 7:12 that "they have hardened their own hearts, and because they wouldn't listen to him when he called out, he was no longer going to listen to their cries, but instead he scattered them to nations where they were strangers, and the land became desolate" (like the widow, if you will).

The first observation to make about this chapter is that if there are any doubts that the main subject matter is worship, then all we have to do is take a closer look at verse 13. In this verse, through Zechariah, God says, "That as he cried, and they would not hear; so they cried, and I would not hear, saith the Lord of hosts." In almost every worship service I have ever attended throughout my life, there has been a call and response between someone behind the pulpit and the congregation. Is there any more that can be said about this than that? God is calling out to his people to "execute true judgment and show mercy and compassion, and not to cause the widow, the fatherless, the stranger and the poor to be oppressed, or to harbor hate against each other."

It is easy for us to give the right response in a worship service because it is usually written down for us to read, but that we read it and then confess it with our lips does not mean that it is a reflection of our own hearts from experiences lived out in our own lives. That is true for both individuals and corporate bodies. It becomes very easy to become complacent in our worship practices. We reach a place where, in rote fashion, we go through the motions of attending church services, singing hymns and praise songs, without any consideration as to whether what we are confessing is true in our own lives. Yet worshipping God by serving others seldom becomes rote or just routine. It can, however, be insincere. Service to others, no matter who they are, family, friend, or stranger, when done only out of a sense of duty or responsibility should not be confused for love.

The next observation is one that I personally find gives me the most pause, but it is the most relevant to this discussion. It reveals to us that our neglect of those such as the physically widowed and the fatherless, as it relates to worship, potentially brings with it consequences of catastrophic proportions—which in this instance is actually what occurred to the people of Bethel. A critical mass, or point of no return, of "impure and defiled worship" had been reached. Notice that God does not say in the last line of Zechariah 7:14 that he had made the pleasant land desolate, but instead he puts the blame completely on the people of Bethel, saying, "They laid the pleasant land desolate." In the New International Version, it more specifically draws the correlation between what Israel is guilty of and this outcome, with this line translated as, "This is how they made the pleasant land desolate."

Second Chronicles 7:14 may be the most often quoted scripture today, as it is quoted more frequently than any other I can think of in recent memory. It is almost as if enough Christians quote it enough times, this will make it come true. It has come to the point where I almost want to scream every time I hear it quoted. The outcome in Zechariah 7 is possibly the best example we have for understanding why God does not guarantee to reverse what has transpired up to the point of no return. Instead, our "impure and defiled worship," once it reaches critical mass, will implode, resulting in even the land becoming a desolate place.

If we fall on our faces and repent but then, once we return to our feet, head down the same path we were on before, have we really repented? And even if we have, will God no longer be willing to listen to us, as we see in Zechariah 7? When God cried out to Israel, they did not listen, so when they finally began to cry out to God, he was no longer willing to listen. A point of no return had been reached—the same point of no return that had been reached when Jesus came and revealed as much when he told the religious leaders that "their house had been left desolate unto them."

This, for me, points to the question of what God really considers to be idolatry. In other words, what comes first, the chicken or the egg? Is it the worship of idols that comes first, or is idolatry in God's eyes really the absence of mercy, compassion, and justice toward those who most represent our own condition apart from Jesus, namely, the widows and the fatherless? If it is the latter, which I believe it to be, then the actual worship of idols (whatever their counterparts are today) is really just symptomatic of the fact that we are choosing to devote the majority of our time and resources on ourselves, both individually and corporately, which in effect is considered by God to be self-worship. Is there really any difference between being self-absorbed and engaging in self-worship? I'll put it another way: the neglect of those such as the widows and the fatherless is, in effect, considered by God to be idolatry/adultery.

Chapter 15: Abomination of Desolation

O ur discussion of the backstory does not end with Jesus's contrasting the faith of the widow who gave all she possessed monetarily with the faith of those who gave only out of the surplus of their wealth. It continues on in the next chapter of the Bible, beginning with Mark 13:1. Right after Jesus reveals the condition of heart that has once again caused Israel's "house to be left unto them desolate," he goes outside the temple with his disciples, and immediately one of them turns to him and marvels at the sheer size of the stones and the appearance of the temple—which is a truly amazing contrast to what Jesus, as God, has just revealed as a heart assessment of the house of Israel: "God judges the heart, but man judges the outward appearances" (1 Samuel 16:7).

It seems to have always been the case, and will always remain a struggle for us as God's people, that outward appearances (e.g., the size of a church's budget, the size and number of a church's buildings, and/or a church's number of members) are mistakenly thought to be signs of Christian success, whereas it is the inward reality of the condition of the heart that is the true indication of whether or not our successful-appearing houses of worship have actually become houses left unto us desolate.

Jesus quickly replies to this disciple, saying not only that the physical building will be turned into a pile of rubble, but also that the self-serving system of worship will crumble with it. Then he sits down on the Mount of Olives, which is opposite the temple, and has a private conversation with four of his disciples, who appear very anxious to know when this destruction is going to take place.

His response to them, though, is not to tell them when this is going to take place but, instead, to admonish them not to be deceived (as Eve was by the Serpent). He says that many will come claiming to be the Christ but that the disciples should not be taken in by those people.

How can this not be understood in any other way except in the context of what Jesus, as God, has just revealed to his disciples inside the temple, namely, what he had just based his assessment of the heart condition of Israel on? Does this not give us a clear understanding of the characteristics of deception Jesus was telling his disciples to be on their guard against? He told them that their failure to understand what he had just revealed to them, which stood in stark contrast to him and thus to God, would lead them to be easily deceived when he was no longer with them.

Only then does Jesus tell them not an exact date, but what to look for as signs of the physical reality of the temple's destruction. These are all warnings that most Christians today are very familiar with: "wars and rumors of wars and nations rising up against nations" (Mark 13:8). But then Jesus quotes something from Daniel the prophet: "But when you shall see the abomination of desolation standing where it ought not, then let them that be in Judaea flee to the mountains" (Mark 13:14).

The Gospel of Matthew account is similar, but instead of saying, "the abomination of desolation standing where it ought not to," Jesus tells his disciples, "It stands in the holy place." But in the only other Gospel account where this same conversation has been recorded, Luke 21:20, Jesus tells them, "When you see Jerusalem being surrounded by armies, you will know that its desolation is near" (NIV).

Many interpret Jesus's speaking of "the abomination of desolation standing where it should not, or in the holy place" to mean that something will take place during the end times when the Antichrist appears. Just as a point of clarification, the only place the "abomination of desolation" should never stand is in the church, "as judgment will always begin with God's household" (I Peter 4:17 NIV).

Yet when we also include the third account, Luke 21:20, it becomes apparent that Jesus is speaking to the disciples both about that present day, saying that the "abomination of desolation" is already "standing where it should not, in the holy place," as a present spiritual condition reality, and about a future reality, a physical condition yet to come.

Let us know two things: (1) Jesus has already said in Mathew 23:28, "Behold, your house is left unto you desolate" (KJV), to describe the present spiritual condition reality. (2) In Luke 21:20, Jesus says, "When you see Jerusalem being surrounded by armies, you will know that its desolation is near" (NIV), which we know is something that took place forty years later when the temple was, in fact, surrounded by the Roman army and reduced to rubble.

Before I had an understanding of what I now refer to as Widow, Bride, and Marriage Theology, any grasp I might have thought I had on what Jesus meant by "the abomination of desolation" was at best weak. Once I began to clearly see the way this theological tract ties the entirety of scripture together without corrupting the simplicity that is in Jesus, the meaning became obviously apparent.

Abomination simply means "idolatry" and is synonymous with "adultery." The Greek word for *desolation* used here is *erēmōsis*, which means "a making desolate, desolation."[19] It is used only three times in the entire New Testament, with all three instances occurring in the three Gospel accounts already mentioned in paragraphs 6, 7, and 9 of this chapter. As has already been discussed in chapter 1, the Old Testament word for *widow* is *'almanah*, which, in addition to being translated as the word *widow*, has been translated as a "desolate house or desolate palace." And metaphorically, it is translated as "a state bereft of its king."[20]

This was not the first time the "abomination of desolation was standing where it should not"; it had occurred repeatedly throughout Israel's history. The best example, perhaps, is Zechariah 7, which ties the neglect of those such as widows and the fatherless to worship, with both the fault and the consequences of the "pleasant land being made desolate" placed squarely on Israel's shoulders. In fact, the "abomination of desolation standing where it should not" (and again, the only place it should not stand is in the church) will continue to occur every time a critical mass is reached as a result of our worship being impure and defiled rather than pure and undefiled. What we have failed to realize is that when a critical mass of impure and defiled worship is reached and the outcome is that of desolation, or "our house being left unto us desolate," what it literally means is that by our not caring for those such as the widows and the fatherless, both our house and the very land itself will become like the widow: desolate. Just because our houses of worship outwardly appear prosperous does not mean or ensure that on a spiritual level they are not desolate.

Chapter 16: Bride Cup

Mathew 26:29 reads, "But I say unto you, I will not drink henceforth of this fruit of the vine, until that day when I drink it new with you in my father's kingdom" (KJV). Although this might not seem like a passage that has anything to do with widows or the backstory leading up to the discussion of Acts 6:1–6, in the context of God's promise to send a Savior, fulfilled through the person of Jesus, who sacrificed his life so that we might be delivered from our spiritual condition of widowhood, redeemed as his bride, and restored with him in paradise, it has as much to do with the significance of what took place in these six verses as everything else that has been presented thus far.

What Jesus says to his disciples in this verse in Matthew happens in the upper room when he is serving the Passover meal to them the night he is betrayed. What precedes this, though, is what Protestants call Holy Communion, or the Lord's Supper, and what Anglicans call the Eucharist. The Passover meal itself, including what each element now symbolizes, is modeled on Jesus's instructions to his disciples during the meal. Matthew 26:26–28 reads, "And as they were eating, Jesus took bread, and blessed it, and brake it, and gave it to the disciples, and said, eat; this is my body. And he took the cup, and gave thanks, and gave it to them, saying, Drink ye all of it; For this is my blood of the new testament, which is shed for many for the remission of sins" (KJV).

However, since we have lost sight of what we are really meant to understand about what Jesus tells his disciples as he breaks the bread and passes the cup of wine during the Passover meal, Holy Communion today, which is meant to be a celebration, has turned into what feels more like a memorial service. This is ironic, since the Passover meal is, in effect, a memorial service of the first Exodus, when God delivers the Jews out of bondage from Egypt, as well as a foreshadowing of the second exodus, when Jesus, through his death, burial, and resurrection, brings to us *deliverance, redemption, and restoration.*

If you are unfamiliar with what takes place in a traditional Passover meal, there are four cups of wine drunk throughout the course of it. Each of the four cups is meant to represent one of God's promises to the Israelites as stated in Exodus 6:6–7. The first two cups of wine drunk before the meal represent God's promises to the Jews to "take them out of Egypt and to deliver them out of slavery."

The third cup drunk with the Passover meal represents redemption: "I will redeem you with a demonstration of my power." Neither this third cup, though, nor the fourth cup, which is meant to represent God's last promise, essentially of restoration, "to acquire them as a people," were drunk by Jesus that night in the upper room.

Based on this traditional order of the cups of wine being drunk during the Passover meal, the first two cups, representing God's deliverance of the Jews out of the hands of the Egyptians and out of the land of Egypt, would have been drunk by Jesus before he shared the meal with his disciples. When Jesus is sitting down with his disciples and serving them the bread and the cup of wine, explaining to them what the bread and the wine now represent, which words, again, are the exact (albeit translated) words repeated every time we celebrate Holy Communion, it would be on the third cup of wine drunk during the Passover meal. He does not drink this third cup, though, so it is right after he gives thanks and passes this cup to his disciples that he tells them that his lips will not touch the fruit of the vine until he drinks it with them in paradise.

The confusion comes between our understanding of what this third cup of wine is meant to represent and the order in which it comes in the Passover meal. When Jesus tells his disciples in Matthew 26:29 that his lips will not touch the fruit of the vine until he drinks it with us in his Father's kingdom, he is talking about the fourth cup of wine, which represents restoration. This is also the cup that we will drink from with Jesus when we are joined with him at the marriage feast of the Lamb, when we are fully restored to paradise.

So the question now becomes this: if Jesus has already drunk the first two cups of wine, representing God's deliverance, and if the fourth cup of wine is to be drunk by him with us when we are joined with him in paradise, when does he drink the third cup, which represents God's redemption?

Once we realize that Jesus didn't drink the third cup during the Passover meal, it really shouldn't be that hard for us to figure out when he drank from it. It should now be obvious that the cup Jesus asks his Father to take away from him when he is "watching and praying in the garden of Gethsemane" just before he is arrested, is this third cup. Jesus, knowing the suffering that he would have to go through in order to drink this third cup, the cup of salvation/redemption, asks God in Matthew 26:39, "O my Father, if it be possible, let this cup pass from me: nevertheless not as I will, but as thou wilt." Remarkably, in the same instant that these temptation-filled words leave Jesus's lips, he recants them and fully submits to his Father's will.

By contrast, some of the same disciples to whom Jesus had served the Passover meal, and afterward in the garden had asked to "come watch and pray with him least they fell into temptation" (Matthew 16:41), fall asleep while he remains awake. When the hour arrives for him to be arrested, his disciples who slept instead of watching and praying succumbed to the temptation of fear, whereas Jesus does not. Not only does he know his Father's will, but also with his whole being he is willing to submit to it. And his Father's will is for him to drink this third cup through the sacrifice of his own life, something he knows is God's singular purpose for sending him, whereas his disciples still have not yet grasped this. They are still in slumber mode, so to speak.

And finally, in the Gospel of John (19:28-30), we read, "Jesus knowing that all things were now accomplished, that the scripture might be fulfilled, saith, I thirst" (KJV). Doesn't it become even more obvious what Jesus's thirst is really for now that we know this third cup that Jesus did not drink is the one he will drink through the act of offering up his own life? It would be ludicrous for us to think that Jesus's thirst at that moment had anything to do with the quenching of his physical thirst, especially when you consider what Jesus tells the Samaritan woman at the well in John 4:14: "But whoever drinks the water I give them will never thirst. Indeed, the water I give them will become in them a spring of water welling up to eternal life." We know that Jesus is the source of this living water.

Of course, those who were attending to Jesus at that moment and heard him say, "I thirst," mistakenly thought he was speaking of physical thirst. His thirst, however, was not physical. Rather, his thirst was to drink from the cup that only a few hours prior he had asked his Father to take away from him. That Jesus already knew that he was about to give up his ghost only adds to this case being made that his thirst was not a physical one.

Also, he was given sour, or spoiled, wine. Based on the paradise that Jesus, through the sacrifice of his life, is about to open the door to for us to enter, by comparison this sour wine, essentially, might also represent what all things might be likened to that we consider to be the very best things that this world has to offer. It also remains true to what Jesus said at the Last Supper, that his lips would not touch the fruit of the vine until he was with them/us in paradise.

Plainly stated, the four cups of wine drunk during the Passover meal symbolizing *deliverance, redemption, and restoration* are now all represented by a single cup, the cup we drink when celebrating Holy Communion. This cup, though, does not only represent the cup of salvation; it also represents for us the bride cup. The two are, in fact, synonymous. Jesus ultimately came to redeem a bride. That bride we know to be his church. Thus, given the sacrifice of Jesus's life, the drinking the cup of salvation, he now offers this same cup to all who would accept his proposal of marriage.

Because of Adam and Eve's sin, we all inherited their fallen condition of *spiritual widowhood*. Jesus, through his death, delivers us from this condition of widowhood and redeems us through our acceptance of his proposal of marriage, thereby making us his bride and giving to us the hope and promise in him that we will one day be fully restored back to paradise at the time of the marriage feast of the Lamb.

So, for us as Jesus's betrothed, celebrating Holy Communion, the Lord's Supper, the Eucharist, should equally symbolize both the celebration of the new covenant relationship we have with God through Jesus as his bride and as a time for renewing our marriage vows to Jesus in anticipation of the marriage feast of the Lamb at the end of this age.

And hopefully the relevance of this point being included as part of the backstory leading up to the discussion of the significance of Acts 6:1-6 has not been lost. Without understanding that Jesus came to redeem a bride and that the gospel is essentially a proposal of marriage, it is difficult to understand Paul's warning in 2 Corinthians 11:2–3, "that we might be presented to Jesus as a chaste virgin, and that we not be deceived as Eve was by the Serpent and our minds led away from the simplicity that is in Christ." And what I mean by *difficult* is simply that by not understanding that we are a bride and that we are to remain "chaste as a virgin," the probability that we will understand that our vulnerability as the church/bride, whether we are male or female, is that of Eve and not of Adam, is little to none. History certainly bears this out.

What has been discussed in this chapter, based on these passages in 2 Corinthians, is meant to counter all erroneous understanding relating to it where deception has overtaken us as Christ's bride, which has ultimately prevented us from correctly interpreting the significance of what was really taking place in Acts 6:1–6 and thereby failing to grasp what would cause such an outcome as reported in Acts 6:7 to occur. And this next and final chapter of backstory before discussing Acts 6:1–6 is, in like fashion, intended to further expand on this backstory, again with the hope that everything being presented will ultimately serve to create a picture so complete as to make plain how deceived we have become, which deception has prevented us from being the "pure and undefiled bride" Jesus desires us to be.

Chapter 17: Jesus' Final Act on the Cross

Generally, when speaking to a church group about the scriptural basis for the need to care for widows, I will also usually include the question, "What was Jesus's final act on the cross?" Whether it is with a small group of adults or a high school youth group, rarely is anyone, in my over twenty-five years of asking this question, able to give the right answer. There is a very reasonable explanation for this, and I think it's simply that little or no significance has been attached to either Mary or this event. Obviously, if Mary and the provision that Jesus makes for her as his last act were seen as having more significance, then far more Christians would know the correct answer.

According to the Gospel of John (the only Gospel account that includes this), Jesus's final act on the cross was to entrust the care of his widowed mother to John, the disciple whom he loved (John 19:26–27). The reason that we know this to be Jesus's final act is that immediately following this, John tells us, "Jesus, knowing that all things were now accomplished, that the scripture might be fulfilled, saith, I thirst" (John 1:28 KJV). And as was discussed in the previous chapter, what Jesus thirsts for is to drink from the cup of salvation, or as I have come to refer to it, the bride cup.

Perhaps the problem lies in the way(s) in which we view Mary. Mary has to be the most misunderstood person in the New Testament. Our regard for her includes everything from deification to nullification.

And sadly, at both extremes of this spectrum, she is considered to have played a role of lesser significance than her other roles. And by focusing almost solely on this role, we miss the significance of the other roles she is meant to symbolize for us, which are at least equal to, if not greater than, this lesser role.

The lesser role I am speaking of is that of mother, with a greater role being that of widow, but with the greatest role of all, perhaps, being that of virgin bride. Without a Widow, Bride, and Marriage Theological perspective of scripture, especially as it relates to our relationship with Jesus as his betrothed, it is almost impossible, or so it would seem, to make this connection.

So, before taking a more in-depth look at the significance of Jesus's last act on the cross and discussing why it was essential that he make provision for his mother, specifically because of her condition of widowhood, I think an explanation needs to be made as to why we should look at Mary's role as Jesus's mother as a lesser role.

First, though, let me say that *lesser* is not actually what I believe Mary's role as mother to be as compared to her other roles. But by saying it in this way, I have hopefully stirred enough interest for continued reading so that I may present an expanded view beyond the one that is most typically accepted, thus broadening the scope of understanding for the many roles that should be identified with Mary, roles that are equally as important as that of mother. Understanding these roles will also help us, as Jesus's betrothed, to understand more fully what Jesus really came to do and the way that God sees us now as His Son's bride.

Mary being identified as Jesus's mother is obviously significant, because if she had not been in this role to begin with, this discussion would not be taking place. What I am saying, though, is that it is not to be the only role that we should esteem her for. And it is definitely not one that I believe God wants to overshadow the significance of her other roles or what they are meant to symbolize for us. If you will remember, before Mary was Jesus's mother, she was a virgin bride who found favor with God. And then at some point after Jesus's birth, she also became a widow. Perhaps these two other roles are not greater than the role Mary has as being Jesus's mother, but they are certainly both equally as important.

One of the most compelling facts for me in coming to this conclusion is that Jesus never addresses Mary as his mother in any of the Gospel accounts, but instead he always calls her "woman." Even these instances are scarce, with only two recorded: Jesus's last act on the cross in John 19:26–27, and the marriage celebration at Cana where he performs his first miracle, John 2:4. In both cases, though, these instances speak more to the other roles Mary plays than that of Jesus's mother. And, somewhat paradoxically, at the same time, if she were not his mother, she would not be important to us in these significant other roles.

To take it a step further, if God intended for us to uphold Mary's significance as Jesus's mother as the only thing we should regard her for, then wouldn't it stand to reason that Jesus would have called her "Mother" or referred to her as his mother in at least one of the Gospel accounts?

In fact, not only does Jesus never address Mary as his mother, but in the one instance where he clearly has the opportunity to do so, he doesn't do it. Instead, he makes a point of almost disassociating himself from her in that respect. The instance being referred to is in Mathew 12:46–50. It was while Jesus was speaking to a crowd of people and someone told him his mother and brothers were there. Jesus's response was to ask the question, "Who is my mother? and who are my brethren?" Then he turned to his disciples, stretched out his hand toward them, and answered his own question by saying, "Behold my mother and my brethren." He finishes with, "For whosoever shall do the will of my Father which is in heaven, the same is my brother, and sister, and mother" (KJV).

Obviously, Jesus was not being cruel to his mother, just as he was not being derogatory when he addressed her as "woman" in John 2:4 and John 19:26. The Greek word for *woman* used in both instances is *gynē*, which means (1) a woman of any age, whether a virgin, or married, or a widow, (2) a wife, or (3) of a betrothed woman."[21]

By addressing Mary as "woman" rather than Mother, based on

this definition, Jesus is giving us significant insight into the other roles we should equally be identifying with Mary: virgin bride, widow, and betrothed woman. Why? Because those are the exact roles that Jesus was calling our attention to when he called Mary "woman" instead of "Mother." And he wasn't doing it just for himself; he was doing it for us, so that we might truly understand what the simplicity of our relationship to him as his betrothed is based on.

What is perhaps most difficult for us to realize when it comes to Mary and the other roles she symbolizes for us is being able to understand that she is just as much in need of a savior as everyone else. That Mary, once Jesus gave up the ghost and was resurrected, would be equally part of the church and therefore Christ's bride, in the same way as everyone else who accepts his proposal of marriage. Granted, this is really hard to get our minds around, the idea that Jesus, being fully human, is the son of Mary but also, being fully God, is her savior as well as her betrothed. Nonetheless, it is true, and scripture bears out this truth.

For one, this truth is being clearly unveiled (no pun intended) during the wedding feast at Cana, where John tells us that "both Jesus was called, and his disciples, to the marriage" (John 2:2). Additionally, we learn that Jesus's mother was there, because in the very next passage she comes to him to let him know the wine has run out. Jesus's response in verse 4 is, "Woman, what have I to do with thee? mine hour is not yet come" (KJV). Given the definition of the Greek word for *woman* that we just looked at in paragraph 11 of this chapter, we are given great insight into the ways God would have us see Mary in a future sense, as symbolizing for us the church as the bride of Christ.

In fact, this event not only foreshadows the wedding feast that will take place at the marriage of the Lamb but also is consistent with Jesus's own words to his disciples at the Passover meal: "But I say unto you, I will not drink henceforth of this fruit of the vine, until that day when I drink it new with you in my Father's kingdom" (KJV).

As was discussed in the previous chapter, in this last instance Jesus was speaking of the fourth cup of wine drunk during the Passover meal. The cup drunk during this meal represented God's promise to

Israel that once they were delivered out of the hands of the Egyptians, "he would take them to himself for a people" (Exodus 6:7 KJV). Now, when Jesus drinks this fourth cup with us, it will mean that the third part of God's promise (to send a Savior who will deliver, redeem, and restore) to Adam and Eve has been fulfilled. We will no longer "see in a mirror darkly" but will be fully restored and in his presence for all of eternity.

Hopefully, it has now been made clear why Mary playing the role of mother does not make sense in this context. What does make perfect sense is that here she symbolizes for us the church as Jesus's betrothed. Let's look again at the definition of *woman*: (1) a woman of any age, whether a virgin, or married, or a widow, (2) a wife, or (3) of a betrothed woman." Mary, favored of God, was a virgin bride who became a virgin mother and then a wife to Joseph, and she eventually became a widow. Jesus came and offered up his life as the fulfillment of his Father's promise to the fallen Adam and Eve to take away our inherited condition of being spiritually widowed, delivering us from this fallen condition, redeeming us through our acceptance of his proposal of marriage, and restoring us through matrimony.

So, what this essentially means is that Mary not only symbolizes at the wedding in Cana Jesus's betrothed, the church, but also, in a much larger context, serves as our example for being the bride that God desires us to be for his Son "as a chaste virgin" who will not be "deceived as Eve was by the serpent or that our minds be corrupted from the simplicity that is in Christ" (2 Corinthians 11:2–3 KJV).

Perhaps now is a good time to return to the original intent of this chapter, which is to take a more in-depth look at Jesus's last act on the cross, with the purpose being to give us an even more complete backstory for understanding the broad implications of the word *visit* in James 1:27, and see it as an act of "pure and undefiled worship." And in the process, we will broaden the scope of understanding for why the actions taken in Acts 6:1–6 led to the outcomes reported in verse 7. This will hopefully heighten our own expectations for the same, and what we should consider to be naturally occurring outcomes today, rather than the forced ones we work so hard and spend so much time and money to produce, with very little kingdom results to show for our efforts.

Efforts that include words like *marketing* and *branding* that were once used to describe the strategies used by advertising and marketing agencies, and are now used as strategies by churches. Ultimately, producing many of the same results as advertising agencies intend for their clients, especially for attracting more members in order to increase giving (cash flow). As Acts 6:1–6 will demonstrate, though, the only strategy we may really need is simply to visit.

Let's begin, now, by taking a look at the complete text in John 19:26–27 that records Jesus's last act on the cross: "When Jesus therefore saw his mother, and the disciple standing by, whom he loved, he saith unto his mother, Woman, behold thy son! Then saith to the disciple, Behold thy mother! And from that hour that disciple took her unto his own home" (KJV).

And again, by being reminded of the definition for the Greek word for *woman*, it will hopefully become clear to anyone reading this that Mary, at that moment, actually embodied all of the roles that she should be equally regarded for, beginning with her being a virgin bride and ending with her becoming a widow. It was at that very moment, through this final act of Jesus, that God shone a spotlight of such intense brightness so as to leave no doubt that Jesus is the one sent to fulfill his promise to Adam and Eve for sending a savior, who would also be bridegroom and husband, thus forever removing that which had blocked the way for us to reenter paradise.

If the waters are still muddy, or at least a little cloudy, regarding what has been presented thus far as the many equally significant roles that we should see Mary as being in addition to being the mother of Jesus, then this next and final point will hopefully leave no room for doubt as to the significance of these roles and why they are important.

This final point is something that drew my attention during a church service some twenty years ago. Interestingly, this happened while I was reciting the Apostles' Creed, something I had memorized as a young child and had recited who knows how many hundreds, if not thousands, of times before that particular Sunday morning.

What occurred to me that morning that had never occurred to me before was the second line in the creed stating that Jesus was "conceived by the Holy Ghost." As crazy as this might sound, what suddenly hit me was the fact that conception is something that we typically identify with a woman and not a man. For the rest of the service that day, and who knows for how long afterward, I struggled to understand the significance of this, having only heard the Holy Ghost referred to in the masculine, "he," and that he alone, with Mary, was involved in the conception of Jesus.

The word *conceived* just wouldn't leave me alone, though. There had to be more to this than I had come to believe about both Mary's role and the Holy Ghost's role in the conception of Jesus. If there wasn't, then the theory that Mary played other roles, which I have come to believe we should recognize and understand as being equally significant as her role as mother, although highly plausible, was still lacking the irrefutable proof I believed was needed.

So I began to pray and to search through the Gospel accounts of the times before and the times leading up to the conception of Jesus. Finding the scriptural basis for the second line of the Apostles' Creed, which mentions that Jesus was conceived by the Holy Ghost, was fairly easy. I found it in Mathew 1:20: "But while he [Joseph] thought on these things, behold, the angel of the Lord appeared unto him in a dream, saying, Joseph, thou son of David, fear not to take unto thee Mary thy wife: *for that which is conceived in her is of the Holy Ghost*" (KJV, emphasis added).

What I suspected, but what was not as easy to find as this first scriptural reference, was an account of the conception of Jesus that included God the Father as being a participant. And just as I had suspected, the evidence I had been looking for was there. I found it in Luke 1:35, which reads, "And the angel answered and said unto her [Mary], The Holy Ghost shall come upon thee, and *the power of the Highest shall overshadow thee*: therefore also that holy thing which shall be born of thee shall be called the Son of God" (KJV, emphasis added).

Wanting to allay any doubts that might remain regarding to whom "the Highest" is referring in this passage I looked up the Greek word for *Highest* to see if it would provide the final proof I needed. And not surprisingly, the Greek word for *Highest* is *hypsistos*, an adverb, which has as part of its definition "the most high God,"[22] who is always God the Father, thus relieving me of all doubts—and hopefully removing all doubts for anyone else going forward.

Based on this last scripture, Luke 1:35, which reveals to us that both the Holy Ghost and God the Father participated in the conception of Jesus, there is really no other conclusion that can be reached for the role that Mary fulfills as the mother of Jesus except as his surrogate mother. Based on this same passage, it is quite clear that Jesus is to be known as the Son of God, not the Son of the Holy Ghost or the son of Mary. It is abundantly clear that God has fathered Jesus with the Holy Ghost.

Please do not misunderstand my intentions here and think that it has been my purpose to denigrate in any way Mary's role as the mother of Jesus. If anything, Mary should be regarded with even more honor, just not based strictly on her role as the surrogate mother of Jesus. But if we can't get past Mary's role as mother, a role that has obviously overshadowed the significance of all her other roles, then we will probably never be able to fully recognize and understand what God has intended us to understand through Mary as Jesus's last act on the cross. This includes when John tells us immediately after this final act that, in John 19:27, "From that hour that disciple took her unto his own home."

Again, if we can't get past being able to relate to Mary only as the mother of Jesus, then the significance of the point being made when John tells us that Mary's new home is with him is completely lost. It seems obvious, though, that once we realize that Mary in her role as physical widow, which symbolizes our own condition of *spiritual widowhood*, from which Jesus came to deliver and redeem us, as well as in her role as virgin bride, which symbolizes what God desires us to be as Christ's betrothed, we also see that based on these other roles, there is none better suited to symbolize these things for us than Mary. Given all of her respective roles that have been discussed here, along with what is symbolized by Jesus entrusting her care to John, "the disciple whom he loved," this is yet another profound instance that proves who Jesus claims to be, the Son of God. John stating he is taking Mary to his own home also symbolizes what Jesus said to his disciples in John 14:2: "In my Father's house are many mansions: if it were not so, I would have told you. I go to prepare a place for you" (KJV).

I want to conclude this chapter by saying that Jesus's last act on the cross literally gives us a picture of God's promise to send Jesus, the fulfillment of his sending Jesus to sacrifice his own life for us, and the hope that we now have through Jesus, as Savior and Bridegroom, of being with him for all eternity. And all of this was confirmed through the single person of Mary and all the roles that she is meant to represent to us through this last act: widow (deliverance), bride (redemption), and marriage (restoration), which means that Jesus's last act on the cross should be understood by us to be the ultimate act of "pure and undefiled worship."

Chapter 18: Acts 6:1–6

My apologies if it feels a bit like having had to travel from one city to another and back again just to get from the kitchen to the dining room, before finally returning this discussion to the first six verses in Acts 6. It is important to remember, though, that the context of this discussion continues to be rooted in James 1:27, with the focus continuing to be on the word *visit* in relation to outcomes for *deliverance*, *redemption*, and *"God breathing life into."* Hopefully, new insights have been realized along the way relating to the word *visit*, as this applies the actual significance of what was taking place in these first six verses of Acts 6, and why.

First, though, it should be noted that this need arising for a group of minority widows to be included in the daily distribution of food is reported as happening just one-fifth of the way into the twenty-eight chapters of the book of Acts and only four chapters after Pentecost. The fact that the distributing of food to widows is reported as soon as it is in this chapter does not, in and of itself, mean that it should be interpreted as being more significant than anything recorded later on. Yet at the same time, with all of the dots that have been connected in the last five chapters of *Spiritual Widowhood* as backstory, I think that this specific need involving widows to arise so early in the form and function of the emerging church lends more credence to its significance than it might have otherwise.

Going forward with this discussion, it is key to remember Jesus's time in the temple with his disciples (Mark 12), where he points out the contrast between the widow at the altar giving all she had and everyone else at the altar giving out of their surplus. In many ways, this widow represents, through her physical condition of widowhood, the church that Jesus has come to *deliver, redeem, and restore* as his bride. Equally, the other people he draws the disciples' attention to are evidence of the church's actual condition of a "house left desolate," which we should take as meaning that they are just as guilty of "devouring the widows' houses" as the scribes whom Jesus had pointed out to his disciples just prior to this. The scribes, in fact, were there to mock Jesus, along with the chief priests and elders, while he hung on the cross (Mathew 27:41).

It is also important to remember Mary and the provision that Jesus made for her by placing her in the care of John, the disciple whom he loved. She, likewise, physically represents those who are spiritually widowed whom Jesus was about to sacrifice his life for, as well as being the bride that he came to redeem.

Connecting these two events alone as part of the backstory for this need that arises in the first six verses of Acts 6, is it any wonder that this need for these minority Greek widows became an issue of such great concern so soon after Pentecost? It would have been more surprising if this issue had not arisen. It did arise, though, and more importantly it was recorded—and nothing that has been recorded for us in scripture is without significance. The question is, how much significance should be attached to it? I am convinced that this event is so important as to characterize it as being a moment of critical mass regarding the early church's survival. The deception that Jesus repeatedly warned his disciples not to allow in was immediately recognized as such and kept out. And if this was not the first such incident that could be characterized in this way, it certainly was the second one.

The first critical mass moment that threatened the purity of the early church should be considered to be when Ananias and Sapphira (Acts 5:1–10), in much the same way that the Serpent deceived Eve, who then became the deceiver, attempted to deceive the early believers. They truly are likened to those Jesus pointed out to his disciples at the treasury who gave out of their surplus, contrasted with the widow who gave out of all she had. Ananias and Sapphira, like those giving out of their surplus, were hoping through their public show to give the appearance of being all in, in their devotion to God. They can also be likened to the "leaven of the Pharisees" about which Jesus warned his disciples in Luke 12:1 and which he told them was "hypocrisy." Interestingly, the Greek word for *hypocrisy* comes from the root word meaning "a stage actor, someone playing a part, or portraying a character."[23]

Regarding believing in Jesus, all of us have either heard someone else make the excuse or have made the excuse ourselves that we didn't want to do so because Christians are nothing but a bunch of hypocrites. Often our response when someone else makes this claim is to admit that we all may be hypocrites, but God loves us anyway. Yes, God loves us anyway, but whether the "true worshippers that God desires who will worship him in spirit and in truth" is at the same time a church filled with hypocrites is really hard to reconcile as being acceptable to God.

The kind of hypocrisy that Jesus is pointing out in Luke 12:1, has to do with the level of deception that has taken place, a level causing those in leadership who have been deceived to become the deceivers of all those entrusted to their care. So, for us to so easily admit that, yes, the church is full of hypocrites is to say that we have all been deceived and can all be likened to stage actors able to recite our lines from memory when the occasion calls for it, but our actions, and what I mean by actions are our acts of worship, do not fulfill what it truly means to love God with our hearts, minds, and souls, and our neighbors as ourselves.

At the time of the first critical mass moment, because deception had not yet entered in, the believers were so pure in their devotion to Jesus, and their worship was so "pure and undefiled," that the presence of God through the Holy Spirit fully exposes the deceit, and both Ananias and Sapphira, when confronted with the deceit, immediately give up the ghost and fall dead.

Now, this second critical mass moment, which takes place when attention is called to the minority Greek widows being overlooked in the daily distribution of food, is, first of all, the clear indication of successful discipleship training, especially given Jesus's many warnings to his disciples not to be deceived. It is also obvious that the Twelve understood the critical nature of this plea, especially regarding the critical-mass effects that it could potentially have on the purity of the early church.

To provide an illustration, in football, if the offense can't succeed by running the ball up the middle, an alternative strategy is to try an end-around run. Ananias and Sapphira embodied Satan's attempt to bring deception in right through the front door. And when that didn't work, a diversion was created in order to defile the purity of the church and therefore diminish the power of God's presence, as well as the "pure and undefiled" condition of the church going forward.

How else can such an immediate response be explained—and one that provided both an immediate and a long-term solution? In fact, if this had not been the response of the Twelve, in all probability, at that very moment, the church that Jesus came to redeem may have been irreparably deceived and prevented from becoming the church God desired her to be, "filled with worshippers who worship him in spirit and in truth."

On a practical level, let's take a look at these passages in order to understand what is literally taking place (instead of speculating). The very first thing that happened (verse 1) was that some Greek Jews were complaining about their widows being overlooked in the daily distribution of food. This "murmuring" that was going on was obviously brought to the attention of the apostles, who then immediately stopped what they were doing in order to address this critically important concern for those widows' needs.

In Isaiah 1:17, Israel was told, exhorted, and possibly reprimanded, "Learn to do well; seek judgment, relieve the oppressed, judge the fatherless, *plead for the widow*" (KJV, emphasis added). What is literally taking place when this "murmuring" over the neglect of these minority widows reaches the apostles' attention is straight out of this passage of scripture in Isaiah.

The immediate response of the Twelve in Acts 6:2–3 is to call the "multitude of the disciples among them, together and let them choose seven." The seven end up being very broken and humble servants of the Lord who will address this need both immediately and on an ongoing basis. Before these seven are named, though, the Twelve make an interesting statement that has been taken to mean something for which there is really no scriptural basis or precedent to support. It is when they say in the second part of verse 2, after first learning of this need, "It is not reason that we should leave the word of God, and serve tables" (KJV).

Over the years I have heard on many occasions this one verse being quoted by pastors as the basis for their not involving themselves in what is commonly considered to be diaconal ministry. These six verses of Acts 6 are not only their basis for taking this position, but these same verses are cited as the basis for why the office of deacon was originally created to (1) care for widows and (2) relieve pastors so that they can, as the Twelve say in verse three of this same chapter, "give [them]selves continually to prayer, and the ministry of the word" (KJV).

The first thing that needs to be examined is what was meant exactly when the Twelve said in verse 2, "It is not reason that we should leave the word of God, and serve tables." The original Greek word translated as "not reason" is an adjective and simply means "not pleasing or agreeable."[24]

Once again, acknowledging that I am not a Bible scholar, I just don't see how this can be interpreted as a command, especially one that sets the precedent whereby pastors are exempt from personally caring for widows, including waiting on tables. It should also be noted that this adjective is only used a total of four times in the New Testament, but in all three of the other instances it has, in fact, been translated as a form of the word please (i.e. *please, pleased and pleasing*).

Can anything more really be made out of this other than the fact that it just wasn't pleasing or agreeable to the Twelve under the circumstances at that moment to take care of this matter? They also must have realized that taking care of widows would be an ongoing need that in all probability would need to be continually met. This does not mean, though, that they never waited on the widows, either the majority Hebrew widows or the minority Greek widows. They just believed, at that specific juncture and in that specific place, that they needed to continue what they were specifically called to do. If not, then why did Jesus place Mary, his own widowed mother, in the care of one of his disciples? And besides, it should also be pointed out that the office of pastor today has not replaced the office of apostle. If they were, then a case might be made that there is a basis for fulfilling their role as pastor by devoting their time almost exclusively to prayer and ministry of the word. However, if the office of pastor is not the modern day equivalent of the office of apostle, can any such claim really be made for justifying this as their primary role and function to the exclusion of personally caring for those such as the widow.

Perhaps verse 4, "But we will give ourselves continually to prayer, and the ministry of the word," might add to our understanding that a precedent has not been established that exempts pastors from modeling the care of widows. "Will give ourselves continually" has been translated from the Greek word *proskartereo*, a verb, that is used only ten times in the New Testament, including this one.[25]

In other words the disciples saying that they would give themselves continually to the word, and the ministry of the word, would be like any of us saying that "we will continually serve the Lord faithfully" or "we will continually pray without ceasing." There is nothing in this passage that says that every moment of every day the apostles' specific activities will consist of continuous prayer and ministry of the Word any more than we continually serve the Lord faithfully or we continually pray without ceasing. Even Jesus didn't model this. What it does tell us is that at that specific moment in time and at that specific place, it did not please the Twelve to completely put on hold what they were doing, but they were willing, at least, to do it temporarily.

If anyone could make the claim that continual prayer and ministry of the Word was the apostles' sole focus, it would be Jesus, but he was constantly being interrupted and ministering to a broad spectrum of people, including widows, and he never said what the Twelve say here. In fact, Jesus said just the opposite, "that he came to serve and not be served." It is Jesus alone, and not the Twelve, or anyone else for that matter, who is our model in all things when it comes to being his bride and the ways we live it out through acts of worship.

When Jesus entrusts widowed Mary to the care of John, the disciple whom he loved, was he not saying to all of us, including the rest of the disciples, that widows represent our fallen condition and the responsibility lies with all of us to make certain they are cared for? Circumstances may mean that at any given time and place it may not be possible for us to give them hands-on care, regardless of our specific office or calling, but that does not exempt us from making certain that others are positioned to do so. Then when circumstances do allow for it, again regardless of our office or calling, we are to be the ones to "wait on tables." Why? Again, because Jesus is our example in all things, beginning with his coming "to serve and not be served."

By the Twelve taking a break from what they felt called to do at that moment and making provision for not just the care of the Greek widows that one time but also their ongoing care, this was as much an example of "pure and undefiled worship" as was Jesus's last act on the cross. The seriousness of this situation is clearly presented to us by the qualifications of those whom the Twelve chose to oversee the ongoing care of these widows. Verse 3 reads, "Brothers and sisters, choose seven men among you who are known to be full of the Spirit and wisdom. We will turn this responsibility over to them" (NIV).

They could have just said, "Hey, you, you, you, you, you, and you, go deal with this. We don't have time. It's interfering with our high calling, and we just can't be bothered with this right now." That's exactly what Jesus was complaining about to his disciples regarding the scribes who were guilty of "devouring the houses of the widows." Given these qualifications for those who were to be chosen, and especially considering that based on those qualifications Stephen was chosen to be among them, we should be stopped in our tracks to realize the significance of what is actually taking place here.

Especially notable is that Stephen was not only the first New Testament martyr but also the only person whom scripture tells us Jesus stood up in heaven for, the account of which immediately follows the outcomes reported in Act's 6:7 and continues on through to the end of chapter 7. Then beginning with chapter 8, Saul, who would later be called Paul after his conversion, is introduced for the first time as being the one who consented to Stephen's execution. At this moment in the emerging church, who should we consider to resemble most accurately the model that Jesus lived out for us as recorded in the Gospel accounts of his ministry? And who should we think might have influenced Paul's own walk with Jesus the most after his own conversion, Stephen? Or one of the Apostles?

It should also be noted that all who were chosen to ensure that the minority Greek widows were no longer overlooked were also part of the minority Greek culture (they all had Greek names). What makes this significant is the simple fact that majority cultures seldom, if ever, seem willing to share resources (wealth) and authority with a minority culture. More often than not, money is used as power, and when money is used in this way, to wield power, it quenches the Holy Spirit and causes great oppression to those who are the victims.

As a white person, I have come to recognize that I am part of the majority culture in the United States, which gives me privileges that I did nothing to deserve. I have them just by virtue of being born white. Adding to this the fact that I am a man means I am part of the most privileged and powerful demographic in this country, both inside and outside of the church.

Luke 12:8 tells us that "to whom much is given much is expected," which means that I, just by virtue of being born white, nothing I had any control over, am responsible for recognizing this privilege. Thus, the greater burden is on me to serve those who have been born with less privilege. And privilege does not necessarily have anything to do with wealth.

A local African American pastor named Alfred Johnson who has been pastoring the Church of the First Born, a church he started in Chattanooga over thirty years ago, is one of my personal heroes of the faith. Not only does he have a burden for widows and the fatherless, but it has also been the focal point of all his ministry outreach for most of the existence of the church he pastors.

Whenever Widows Harvest Ministries hosts a short-term mission group, part of what is included in their time of serving together with us is a discussion led by Pastor Johnson on race and faith. The demographics of most of these groups are generally white suburban middle-class high school and college-age students, along with their adult leaders. In these discussions, Alfred always begins by telling the group what his experiences were growing up as an African American male beginning in the mid-fifties before the civil rights movement. He makes a point of saying that the white people who would come into his neighborhood and share the gospel were the same people he would run into at other settings who would call him derogatory names, stripping him of his dignity and self-worth as a child.

When he was older, though, he was actually led to Jesus by some white college students he was trying to torment, but they refused to show any anger or hatred toward him. Over time, God softened Alfred's heart, allowing him to forgive the white people for the deep-seated hurt they caused him. He continues to be used mightily by God, not only for kingdom advancements but also by taking the time for people like me and the students I bring in order to help us see and understand the privileges we enjoy just by being born into the majority culture.

One of the things in particular that Alfred shares is something I find to be one of the most disturbing realities that a minority culture faces and that someone in the majority culture will never have to face if they choose not to: that a white person in the United States, especially in the South, can avoid being around black people if they choose to. This is not a choice, however, that black people have, being able to avoid white people, especially when it comes to employment and anything else associated with personal economic advancement.

This reality is easily proven just by looking at where most of the churches of the majority culture are located and where white people live, work, dine out, and spend their leisure time. This fact is not lost on the people of minority cultures, especially when the choice is made by those of the majority culture to stop passing by on the other side of the road and, instead, to head directly toward the people and areas of greatest need. The potential impact this will have is far greater than most people of the white majority culture will ever be able to imagine, especially as long as they continue to succumb to their own fears. It isn't hate that is the opposite of love; it is fear. As 1 John 4:18 tell us, "Perfect love drives out fear" (NIV).

The reason for bringing this up in this discussion is that, as I have already said, I am a white male, which again means I was born into the most privileged class of people in this country. Born in 1956, I did not go to my first integrated school until 1967, when I was in the sixth grade and our family moved to Athens, Georgia. I can still clearly remember, before then, separate drinking fountains and bathrooms, and how all of that changed after the civil rights movement. I was also aware that the laws being changed did not affect people's attitudes or the hardness of their hearts. And although I was still quite young in the 1960s, I personally witnessed this to be particularly true of many of those claiming to be Christ's betrothed.

Jumping ahead almost twenty years to 1985, I, at age twenty-nine, along my wife, moved to Chattanooga, her first time living here and my second. Three months after we came to Chattanooga, as I already shared in chapter 1, I was offered a job with a ministry called Inner City Ministries (ICM), which was located in a high-crime, lower-class, predominantly African American urban neighborhood near the downtown area of this city.

Two years later, I would resign from my position at ICM to start Widows Harvest Ministries, where I remain as its servant director. The majority of widows I have been privileged to minister to over the last almost thirty years have been African American, living in predominantly African American–populated urban neighborhoods, many of which also resemble the neighborhood where I first started a ministry to widows.

Coming to a place of finally recognizing the reality of the privileges I have enjoyed on account of one single factor, being born a white male, I think I can now say I have a lot more understanding of the radical nature of the decision of the Twelve not only in choosing the seven minority Grecian Jews out of all of the other disciples, but also in the authority (laying on of hands and praying over them) and the resources given them for both the immediate need to provide food to these minority widows and ensuring their care on a continued basis.

One additional factor that I believe also contributed to the outcome reported in verse 7 is what I have come to call the Job factor. Job said of himself in 29:13, "I caused the widow's heart to sing with joy." When widows' hearts' are "caused to sing with joy," is this anything less than songs filled with praise and thanksgiving to God for his goodness and mercy? I am completely convinced that above all else, God either hears songs filled with praise and thanksgiving coming from the hearts of widows or hears their cries of hopelessness and despair. Based on the example of Job, what do you think we, as God's people, are most guilty of today, being responsible for causing widows' hearts to be filled with joy, or causing their hearts to be filled with hopelessness and despair?

Whether it can be agreed upon as to whether the stated causes in this chapter's discussion were responsible for the profound outcomes reported in Acts 6:7, it is hard to ignore the fact that there had to have been a cause-and-effect relationship between the things recorded as having taken place in the previous six verses that produced this outcome. So, my challenge would be for those who might hold to the more traditional, or what could be considered an institutionally driven, interpretation to try for themselves to either confirm the case that has been presented here or disprove it. The absolutely worst possible thing to do, though, would be to take no action.

And finally, and perhaps most significantly, the action taken by the disciples that was in the spirit of what is meant by "to visit" in James 1:27, producing as outcomes *deliverance, redemption, and God breathing life into*, was ultimately an act of "*pure and undefiled worship*," perfectly mirroring Jesus's own last and final act when he placed Mary into the care of John, "the disciple whom he loved."

Chapter 19: "To Visit" Revisited

B riefly, I want to share as an illustration of the many outcomes that I have personally witnessed over the years, one that stands out in particular that just started out as another simple routine visit with a widow.

As much as I desire to share the actual name of this widow who became so dear to me, I won't disclose who she was, for the same reason that I wouldn't put a widow up in front of potential supporters to testify to all that we had done for her. Whether in a widow's life or in her memory after she has passed away, it has always been important to me never to exploit the widows we serve, and to treat them with the highest level of respect in order to preserve the dignity they deserve. For this reason, I will refer to this dear widow as Sarah Stinson.

The first time I met Sarah Stinson was when I went to visit her in her home. What prompted this visit was a call she had made several days before seeking my help for painting the exterior of her house. After my initial brief visit, when she had invited me in and offered me a seat in her nicely furnished living room, she accompanied me outside to my car, which was parked in her driveway. As I was about to get in my car and leave, it occurred to me to ask her how she liked to be addressed, as Mrs. Stinson, Ms. Sarah, or just Sarah? Her response really caught me off guard; it wasn't at all what I was expecting. And although, at the time, the significance of her reply was not lost on me, it would still be years until I realized how truly profound it actually was.

Sarah's response to me when I asked how she would like to be addressed was, very simply and yet quite profoundly, "I don't care what you call me. It's how you treat me that matters." Later on, as my friendship with Sarah grew, she also shared something her parents had instilled in her from a very young age, and that was to love everyone no matter what they do to you or how they treat you. What I found equally profound about her sharing this with me was that I believed this to have been true in her own life more than in the life of anyone else I had ever known.

Then one day, while I was visiting with Sarah and we were sitting around her kitchen table, she began to share things with me about her upbringing that she had never mentioned before. And the more she shared about her past, the more I kept thinking about her words to me the first time I met her: "I don't care what you call me. It's only how you treat me that matters." Later on, I would also recall that her parents had told her to love everyone no matter what they do to you or how they treat you.

Sarah told me that day that her parents had been sharecroppers down on a farm in a rural part of Alabama. As a child of 11, she had begun working, doing ironing, for the family who owned the land her family both lived on and farmed. When I asked how they had treated her, she cautiously told me they treated their yard animals better than they had treated her. Then she told me that a few years later when she was a teenager her father had been murdered by a transient (she called him a hobo). Her father had stepped between another man, who was his friend, and this transient in order to break up an argument between them. The transient, who had already drawn a gun, shot and killed her father instead of her father's friend. John 15:13 immediately came to mind: "Greater love hath no man than this, that a man lay down his life for his friends" (KJV).

When I asked if the transient was arrested and punished for murdering her father, she didn't say anything at first. Then, with an uncomfortable smile, barely hiding the pain it was obvious she still felt, even though this had happened over fifty years ago, she said, "No, he wasn't," which were words filled with an almost unbearable sadness. In both my ignorance and feelings of outrage, I needed to know and to understand why, and so I asked her. Looking down as if staring at her father at the time of his murder, she again spoke quietly, solemnly, and sadly, but miraculously without any hint of bitterness or hatred. Then, quite matter-of-factly, she said the words that I can still hear her saying as I write this: "Because he was white." And I understood immediately that it was because I was white that she was telling me this, but I still didn't know why.

There was what seemed to be a long period of silence after that. I had no idea what to say, or if I could say anything. Sarah was the one who finally interrupted the silence. And it was then, when she spoke, that I could tell that all she had told me had taken years of building trust that I hadn't even known needed to be built. I was also aware that even then she wasn't completely sure how I would react as a white person, as a white man, to what she revealed to me about her life. There must have been some sense of confidence on her part, though, because of what she finally told me, which turned out to be not merely an interruption of the silence but a complete shattering of it.

Sarah, who was in her mid-seventies at the time, then told me that given all that we had done to help her over the years, like painting her house, replacing her roof, and mowing her grass, as well as her involvement in the widow's prayer ministry, it was the first time in her entire life that she had felt like she was considered to be fully human by white people.

I still think about Sarah and what she told me about herself that day, and how it all began with something so seemingly simple as a visit. My primary motive for having done so was rooted in James 1:27, which had instilled in me the desire to show the same unconditional love I had received from God, who sent his only Son to visit all of us in our distress-filled condition of spiritual widowhood, a love that I recognize I don't deserve, nor does anyone else, but that we are all equally and freely invited to receive.

Chapter 20: The Fatherless

Perhaps more than enough has been said about the significance of the verb *to visit* in James 1:27 and the outcomes in Acts 6:7. Therefore, the next part of this phrase to examine in James 1:27, immediately following the verb *to visit*, is "*the fatherless*." In most translations other than the King James Version, though, the word that is most commonly used is *orphans*. The original Greek word for *the fatherless* is *orphanos*, which easily explains why the most commonly used word for its translation is *orphans*. This Greek word, an adjective, is actually *of unknown origins*, and means "bereft of a father, of parents; (a) of those bereft of a teacher, guide, guardian; (b) orphaned."[26]

The only other time that this word is used in the entire New Testament is in John 14:18, when Jesus tells his disciples, "I will not leave you comfortless: I will come to you" (KJV). Right after he says this, he tells them in the next verse that he is going away "and they will see him no more." What Jesus is literally telling them is not to worry that he is going away, because he promises that he will not leave them bereft.

Only the King James Version translates this word as *comfortless*. In most other translations, the word *orphans* is used. One exception is the Revised Standard Version, which translates *orphanos* in this passage as the word *desolate*. Whatever word is used, though, *comfortless, fatherless, desolate*, or *orphans*, all could be considered to describe some aspect of the definition given above for being bereft on a spiritual, physical, or emotional level.

The shortest distance between two points is a straight line, and you can, in my mind, draw a straight line between John 14:18 and James 1:27. They are speaking, in principle, about the same thing. The physical condition of widowhood and being fatherless both speak to our spiritual condition of widowhood and fatherlessness apart from Jesus. In the same way that God the Father promised to send a savior/bridegroom, Jesus is promising his disciples to send the Holy Spirit to comfort them/us in his absence. Both widowhood and fatherlessness, by definition, exemplify the condition of being bereft either of a husband (in the case of a widow) or a father or parents (in the case of the fatherless), as well as a teacher, guide, or guardian.

There is one difference, I believe, between the condition of widowhood and the condition of fatherlessness, though. Our spiritual condition of widowhood must be taken away first before we are adopted into God's family as his children. In other words, when we accept the Gospel, Jesus's proposal of marriage, we are no longer spiritually widowed in that we are now betrothed to him. At the moment we are betrothed to Jesus, we are also adopted into God's family as his children, meaning that we are no longer spiritually fatherless either.

Pastor Alfred Johnson, first mentioned in chapter 19, works with over a hundred youth each year of various ages through his church's MVP youth discipleship and enrichment ministry. He has told me that the greatest percentage of these youth come from single-parent families. In most cases, the parent raising them is their mother, who, according to scripture, should be considered by us to be a widow. Alfred tells me, though, that if he only works with fatherless kids, he may or may not ever meet their mothers. But if he begins by working with a widowed mother first, he will always encounter her kids. The MVP youth ministry, as a priority, works with kids.

Widows Harvest Ministries (WHM) does not work with either of these two groups (younger widows/single mothers and the fatherless), but instead works almost exclusively with older widows, the demographic that God has clearly called us to serve. Many times over the years I have tried to connect our older widows with younger single-mother widows, but it has never worked out. It is not always easy to get people to understand, especially younger widows with children at home, why we primarily work with older widows. For what should be obvious reasons, the dynamics are completely different when children are involved. That is a completely different ministry. I am very thankful for ministries like MVP that minister to so many fatherless kids. It is these same young widowed mothers, who are not even recognized as scripturally defined widows, who have many of the greatest societal struggles and consequently suffer the most regarding the needs that pile up in their lives almost every day, with many of them going unmet.

It seems like in almost every major city across the United States today, gang-related crime is escalating both in the number of crimes as well as the intensity of violence. This is certainly true in Chattanooga, Tennessee, the city where WHM is located. In recent years, there have been reports listing statistics as high as 90 percent of all youth who end up in prison as adults grew up without a father in the home. It doesn't take much research to also figure out that gang members committing most of the violent crimes (usually shootings) in cities like Chattanooga are also from fatherless homes.

As the church, the betrothed of Jesus, the question is, do we have a gang problem in the United States today, or does the problem really lie in our own neglect of the ever-increasing needs of the widows and the fatherless in our midst? If we do, in fact, have a widow and fatherless crisis in our lower-income communities that is being overlooked and uncared for by God's people, isn't this a strong indication that what we really have, as the root problem, is a worship issue?

And at the heart of this worship issue is really the fact that we have come to define worship based almost solely on our worship-service-centered faith practices, with the effect being the absence of both the necessity and the urgency of worshipping God by visiting those who physically represent our own spiritual condition apart from Jesus. Because, once again, our worship is considered by God as being either "pure and undefiled" or "impure and defiled," with the former leading to restoration and the latter leading to desolation.

In Exodus 22:22-24, God issues a stern warning to Israel when he tells them, "You shall not afflict any widow, or fatherless child. If you afflict them in any way, and they cry at all unto me, I will surely hear their cry; And my wrath shall wax hot, and I will kill you with the sword; and your wives shall be widows, and your children fatherless"(KJV). Doing nothing at all can cause as great an affliction and/or oppression as intentionally seeking to do harm. And the neglected widows and the fatherless, not only in Chattanooga but also around this country and many other parts of the world, might be quick to agree with such a claim.

Chapter 21: "And"

T he next to last word in this greatly expanded interpretation of James 1:27 is the word *and*. A word that does not appear in the original Greek text but that has been added in most Bible translations, with two exceptions, Young's Literal Translation (published in 1862)[27] and the Darby Bible (published in 1867).[28]

The King James Version, which has added the word *and*, differs, as do a number of other translations, by adding a comma after the word *this* in the first line: "Pure religion and undefiled before God and the Father is this, To visit the fatherless and widows in their affliction, (and) to keep himself unspotted from the world."

Other translations, including the New International Version, put a colon after the word *this*, treating what follows as a list. When a colon is placed there, however, what follows is two separate requirements for fulfilling what God considers to be "pure and undefiled worship:" "visiting the fatherless and widows in their distress, and to keep from being polluted by the world."

The insertion or the removal of the word *and*, you might not think would make that much of a difference, but what happens when we remove the word *and*, and leave out the colon as the King James Version does? This passage then reads, "Pure religion and undefiled before God and the Father is this, to visit the fatherless and widows in their affliction to keep himself unspotted from the world." And I believe, by inference, it is more than reasonable to conclude that this be understood as, *in order* "to keep himself unspotted from the world."

Perhaps in the reader's mind, this still reads as a list with two requirements, but if we look at this last line of James 1:27, "and to keep himself unspotted from the world," as something additional to "visiting the widows and the fatherless in their distress," the problem lies with context. Apart from this passage, the directive becomes something that is subjective, so much so that each generation throughout the span of church history has composed, and will continue to compose, their own list(s) of dos and don'ts of what it means to "keep himself unspotted by the world." If asked, each of us no doubt could also easily compose our own personal list of what this might include. I know that I could. But what was once a very long list has now become quite short, and is based on this passage and has only one imperative: "to visit the widows and the fatherless in their affliction."

Proverbs 21:2–3 reads, "Every man's way is right in his own eyes, But the Lord weighs the hearts. To do righteousness and justice is desired by the Lord more than sacrifice" (NASB).[29]

These lists that we might come up with for what we believe will keep us from being polluted by the world really have everything to do with us and our being tempted to use our positions of authority to exercise power and control over those entrusted to our care. And yet everything that Jesus said and did as an example for us had to do with taking our eyes off of ourselves. The fulfillment of what it means to love God with our hearts, minds, and souls, and to love our neighbors as ourselves, is just that. By fulfilling both of these commandments, we are emptied of self, because our purpose becomes that of serving God and others rather than serving self. And serving the widows and the fatherless, which represents our own spiritual condition apart from Jesus, is the most pure and undefiled evidence for revealing where the desires of our heart truly lies.

Even just as a point of logic, why would James present the first two-thirds of James 1:27 in an unmistakably clear way and the last third in a completely ambiguous way, leaving it wide open for subjective interpretations? Wouldn't it make far more sense if this last line had to be interpreted in the context of what the rest of the passage tells us, and then in the context of the complete book of James, and finally in the context of the entire Bible? Without a Widow, Bride, and

Marriage Theological understanding of the Bible, it would seem that the significance of James 1:27 cannot help but be diminished, with the consequence being that this last line, "to keep from being polluted by the world," completely overshadows "to visit the fatherless and the widows in their affliction."

One further note, and what I consider to be irrefutable evidence for supporting this argument is found in I Timothy 5. In verse 4 of this chapter Paul writes, "But if a widow has children or grandchildren, these should learn first of all to put their religion into practice by caring for their own family and so repaying their parents and grandparents, for this is pleasing to God" (NIV). Skipping ahead to verse 8, but remembering that it is in the same context as verse 5 for our need to care for widows, is what I believe especially provides us with the irrefutable evidence for this last line in James 1:27 being meant to be understood solely in the context of the first part of this same passage, "Anyone who does not provide for their relatives, and especially their own household, has denied the faith and is worse than an unbeliever" (NIV).

Perhaps, after the final word in this verse to be looked at as this discussion on James 1:27 comes to a close, will hopefully remove all doubts about the point being made in this chapter as being irrefutable, that "visiting the fatherless and the widows in their affliction" not only keeps us from being polluted by the world, but also is one of the most critical standards by which we are to assess ourselves for determining our present condition as the church.

Chapter 22: "To Keep"

This infinitive verb, *to keep*, in the last line of James 1:27 is actually translated from the single Greek word, *téreó* and means, "to attend to carefully, take care of; (a) to guard; (b) metaphorically, to keep, one in the state in which he is; (c) to observe; (d) to reserve: to undergo something."[30]

Back in chapter 11, the point was made that God's purpose for Adam when he put him in the garden was "to dress it and to keep it." "To dress it," if you will remember, is the translation of the word *'abad*, which means "to serve," or "to labor" in the context of worship. "To dress the garden" was considered by God to be worship.

However, what was not discussed at that time was the Hebrew word for "to keep it," which may come as no surprise at this point that it does not differ in meaning in any significant way from the meaning of the Greek word for "to keep" in James 1:27.

The Hebrew word for, "to keep it," is shamar, also a verb, and means, according to Strong's Concordance, "to hedge about (as with thorns), to guard, protect."[31] Essentially, to maintain the order of by not letting anything harmful or deceptive enter in, as opposed to guarding someone, or some thing, in order to keep it from escaping.

Again, the point being, that the relationship between "to dress it" and "to keep it" is that worship, according to God's mandates for us, is the maintaining of his order of things, which is what it means "to keep it." We cannot "keep it," that is, maintain the order of, if we are not dressing it according to God's specific mandates. If we were to apply "to dress it and to keep it" to James 1:27, "to dress it" would be "visiting the fatherless and the widows in their distress as acts of pure and undefiled worship" and "to keep it" would be maintaining this prescribed order by not allowing deception to enter in and disrupt it.

Additionally, the Greek word for *to keep* also figuratively means "to keep unmarried."[32] In other words, when we do not carry out or fulfill God's mandated order for what he considers to be "pure and undefiled worship," this implies that we not only are living in an adulterous relationship with the world but also have forgotten what Jesus has done on our behalf through the sacrifice of his own life; i.e. that Jesus came to deliver and redeem us from our condition of spiritual widowhood and fatherlessness, giving us the hope of full restoration in the process. Again, making this interpretation completely consistent with what was discussed about I Timothy 5:8 at the end of the last chapter, for "Anyone who does not provide for their relatives, and especially their own household, has denied the faith and is worse than an unbeliever" (NIV). And I would further state that I believe this passage to be speaking not only to the individual responsibilities we have for our own physical families and households, but also for the extension of those same responsibilities to insure the care of our spiritual families and households of faith (churches) as well.

This case can be further argued by again looking at 2 Corinthians 11:2–3: "That I might present you as a pure virgin to Christ. But I am afraid that just as Eve was deceived by the serpent's cunning, your minds may somehow be led astray from your sincere and pure devotion to Christ" (NIV). Again, based on a Widow, Bride, and Marriage Theological perspective of the Bible, the evidence is far more compelling that the last line of James 1:27 is telling us, that fulfilling what God considers to be "pure and undefiled worship, visiting the fatherless and the widows in their distress" keeps us from being polluted by the world—not some other, subjective list that seems right in our own eyes at any given place and point in time throughout both church and biblical history.

For the sake of argument, in addition to "visiting the fatherless and the widow in their distress," let's consider that this last line is speaking to us of a list, regardless of how subjective it might be. The first thing that seems to always happen as part of the natural progression for maintaining a system that ensures the purity of the church is to make central to that system a worship service, which generally will require, at some point, the acquisition of a building, and the sooner the better. Without a building, and preferably one that is owned by the congregation, the conclusion would appear to be that it is far more difficult than we think, or perhaps even impossible, to ensure the purity of the church. If this comes across as sarcasm, that was not the intention. A worship service and the necessity for having a building in order to legitimize it for us as an established and credible church historically would almost appear to be a Divine requirement.

It is clear, as Jesus and his disciples are leaving the temple, how Jesus views this temple as the focal point of their worship-service-centered faith based on the remarks made by one of his disciples in Mark 13:1: "...Look, Teacher! What massive stones! What Magnificent buildings!" And then Jesus replies, "Do you see all these great buildings? Not one stone here will be left on another; every one will be thrown down" (NIV). And Jesus is not just speaking of the physical building being reduced to rubble (which literally happened forty years later); he is speaking of the entire system that revolves around a building. A building seems to always have the effect of redefining worship by basing it on our worship-service-centered practices rather than on scripture. And such a system also always seems to result in pride and arrogance clouding our ability to discern the subtle effects of deception creeping in, which ultimately always seems to lead to the "devouring of the widows' houses."

We read in Acts 17:24, "The God who made the world and everything in it is the Lord of heaven and earth and does not live in temples built by human hands" (NIV). This certainly is a reaffirmation of Mark 14:58, where the disciples recall what they heard Jesus say with regard to this: "We heard him [Jesus] say, I will destroy this temple that is made with hands, and within three days I will build another made without hands." Furthermore, there are three additional verses that tell us that we who are betrothed to Jesus are now, individually, considered by God to be his temple:

- "Don't you know that you yourselves are God's temple and that God's Spirit dwells in your midst" (1 Corinthians 3:16 NIV)?
- "If anyone destroys God's temple, God will destroy that person; for God's temple is sacred, and you together are that temple" (1 Corinthians 3:17 NIV).
- "Do you not know that your bodies are temples of the Holy Spirit, who is in you, whom you have received from God? You are not your own; you were bought at a price. Therefore honor God with your bodies" (1 Corinthians 6:19-20 NIV).

In fact, Jesus, providing what appears to be a foreshadowing of the building—that is, worship-service-centered faith—being reduced to rubble, tells his disciples in Matthew 18:20, "For where two or three are gathered together in my name, there am I in the midst of them"(KJV). Once, I actually heard this quoted as the justification for the maintaining of our building-centered and worship-service-centered practices, the assertion being that this passage guarantees that when we are gathered together in Jesus's name, he will be in our midst. Yet we know full well that the Holy Spirit can be quenched, because we are warned in 1 Thessalonians 5:19, "Quench not the spirit." If it were not possible to quench the Spirit, then why be given this warning not to do so? Just because we are two or more gathered together in Jesus's name, and just because that gathering is taking place in a church building as a worship service, does not ensure that our worship actions, or rather inactions, outside of this setting have not caused God's Spirit to be quenched.

Isn't that essentially what God reveals to Israel through Zechariah, in Zechariah 7:9–10, which was discussed in chapter 14, namely, that God questions whether the people of Bethel were fasting and eating unto him, because they were not fulfilling what God considered to be the "execution of true judgment, and showing mercy and compassions every man to his brother: and oppress not the widow, nor the fatherless, the stranger, nor the poor; and let none of you imagine evil against his brother in your heart" (KJV)? Isn't it true that because Jesus tells his disciples before he is even arrested that he will be in their midst when just "two or three are gathered together in his name," that it would also stand to reason that prior to the time of his death and resurrection that God would have been in the midst of those who gathered in his name?

Yet Jesus also said to the scribes and Pharisees in Matthew 23:38, "Behold, your house is left unto you desolate," essentially meaning that God had left the house. Jesus should know, because he is God, and this conversation is taking place outside of the temple and they don't even recognize him. Jesus also taught in Matthew 11:17 "Is it not written, My house shall be called of all nations the house of prayer but you have made it a den of thieves." Which also raises the question today that if our own churches are not considered by God to be houses of prayer, would they then, likewise, be considered by him to have become "a den of thieves?"

And in yet another instance, Jesus says, "Every kingdom divided against itself is brought to desolation; and a house divided against a house falleth" (Luke 11:17). This last verse may be the most poignant one of all. If ever it could be said that the church is divided and headed toward, if it has not already reached, the abomination of desolation, standing where it should not, it could be said of the church in the United States today (not to be confused with political and civil America). The sin that will cause the church to come tumbling down has nothing to do with the sin of our nation. In other words, the church's sin is more likely to cause the downfall of the United States, rather than what seems to be the commonly held view that it is the sin of the United States that is bringing about the downfall of the church. What else would explain why we have turned to saving this nation by gaining political and legislative control rather than completely surrendering our lives to Jesus? Therein lies the problem, we, as the church in America today, have so blurred the lines between the 2 that we seem to have justified one by the other, thus making them one in the same. By refusing to recognize our own sin and understanding the consequences that we are now reaping as a result of our sin, the responsibility for our downfall consequently lies entirely with us who claim Jesus as our betrothed.

Paradoxically, though, most of us who consider ourselves to be included in the household of faith would agree that the mandate to care for the widows and the fatherless is an irrefutable scriptural mandate, while at the same time we do not question why the present form and function of our churches leaves both the care of the widows and the fatherless outside of it. Essentially, invalidating this mandate to care for the widows and the fatherless, not by spoken word but by inaction: the absence of the Word being practically applied and carried out.

Perhaps a quote that a fellow servant, Dr. Chris Robinson, pointed out to me several years ago will serve to illustrate far better than I might be able to the dangers that continue to be associated with a building and worship-service-centered faith practices. The following, written in the second century by Hilary of Poitiers, was written to combat the heresies of the Arian Auxentius of Milan:

> One thing I admonish you, beware of the Antichrist. It is wrong that a love of walls has seized you; wrong that you venerate the church of God in roofs and buildings; wrong that beneath these you introduce the name of peace. Is there any doubt that Antichrist will have his seat in them? To my mind, mountains, woods, lakes, prisons, and chasms are safer. For, either abiding in or cast into them, the prophets prophesized. [33]

This quotation actually came from John Calvin's *Institutes of the Christian Religion*, where Calvin is referencing the issue with regard to the "errors about the nature of the church." The church itself becomes the object of worship—a "lurking hydra."[34]

One probable cause for the resurrection of a building becoming central again to worship-service-centered faith practices is what we would now characterize as marketing and branding. Something, as noted earlier in this chapter, the church has become quite successful at. The early church, though, having been persecuted almost since the beginning, forced the early followers of Jesus underground, resulting in its adherents meeting secretly. Once Constantine decriminalized Christianity in AD 313, the church began to flourish out in the open.[35] How did this now legal church begin to compete with the already established pagan religions, though? The pagans had temples, idols, and overall general public visibility. It's not hard to imagine that similar processes, just different venues, were immediately set into motion in order to maximize the effectiveness for fulfilling the *Great Commission*. The church successfully thrived for almost three hundred years without having its brand attached to a building. Unfortunately, for the next seventeen hundred years, that would no longer be the case.

In all probability, today is not the only time in church history that this has been the case that the single greatest expense for a church is its worship service, but it may be the most excessive. When all of the related costs are factored into what a church spends annually for its weekly worship services, just in the United States alone, no doubt is in the billions of dollars. And the church buildings, it should be pointed out, where billions of dollars are tied up, generally are underutilized or empty the majority of the week.

We have justified this, of course, because all of us have been led to believe that such expense is necessary and that we should give to fund it is as if we are giving unto the Lord. Yet those of us who are giving to this cause are also the direct beneficiaries of our giving. As long as this is the case, we will never balk at how much we spend on ourselves as a church, because again, in our minds, we are convinced that we are giving as unto the Lord.

Following the money trail will always give us away, though. "We worship God with our lips, but our hearts are far away … teaching as doctrine the precepts of men." This is especially true when we contrast what has become for us a worship-service-centered faith and Jesus's own words to his disciples in Luke 12:22–34, beginning with, "Do not worry about your life, what you will eat, or your bodies what you will wear. Because life is more than food and the body more than clothes." He then concludes by telling them to store their treasures in heaven, "for where our treasure is, there our heart will be also." Perhaps it is terribly wrong to question the spending of so much money on worship services, but how can we believe that giving to support such an institutionally driven system is storing up anything for us that

God would see as treasure in heaven, when things such as the widows' houses are being devoured all around us every day?

It has been a thought of mine for some time that if Jesus were to return today and see all of the church buildings, many of which cost tens of millions of dollars, not to mention what it costs to maintain them, he would question why they were built for him. Might he then say to us that he thought he had made it abundantly clear that he was going to prepare a place for us in his Father's house?

Perhaps this seems an overly harsh view of what the church has become in the United States today. I can see how the mere suggestion that this might be more accurately the case than not could be highly offensive to a majority of those who confess Jesus as Savior. Maybe coming at this from a different angle, namely the perspective of the widows and the fatherless, will make this claim more plausible.

First, try and imagine how much time was spent participating in and giving money to those ministry opportunities that directly target the plight of the widows and the fatherless by the church in the Unites States, as compared to the amount of money and time spent funding and/or participating in church-held worship services and related activities?

Now consider the following:

- What percentage of all gang members throughout the United States are growing up, or grew up, in single-parent families where the parent was a still-single widowed mother?
- What percentage of all gang members who are committing the most violent crimes, especially murder, do you think are growing up, or grew up, in single-parent families where the parent was a still-single widowed mother?
- What percentage of men in prison today do you believe grew up in single-parent families where the parent was a still-single widowed mother?
- What do you think the total cost is to society for all of those who are growing up, or grew up, in single-parent families where the parent was a still-single widowed mother, after factoring

in all welfare-related costs, all law enforcement costs, all legal system costs, all penal system costs, and all health-care-related costs?

As of 2014, there "were approximately 2.2 million men in either state or federal prisons out of a population of 318.9 million people. African American men made up 37% of this total number."[36] Statistics are, unfortunately, not generally kept of the family background of those who are incarcerated, but the general consensus is that the majority of them came from single-parent families. Interestingly, according to a Pew research poll of 2014, 70.6 percent of Americans claimed to be either Protestant or Catholic.[37]

Obviously, by the time the fatherless end up in prison, crime prevention is too late. Yet we are far more willing to financially support ministries that serve those in prison, as well as to personally visit and minister to those in prison, than we are to support ministries that serve those who if visited during their more formative and impressionable years, might have been prevented from going to prison in the first place. It is more likely than not that fear keeps us from visiting the fatherless and their widowed mothers before they get into trouble because of the color of their skin and/or where they live. Obviously, ministering to those behind bars doesn't present much of a threat to us personally, because prisoners are under lock and key with guards watching over them.

So, is it really all about fear? Or is it a mixture of fear, ignorance, and some unacknowledged struggles with racism? Again, according to 1 John 4:18, the opposite of love is fear. "There is no fear in love, and those who fear are not perfected in God's love, because we associate fear with punishment." Something else we don't think about regarding fear is that it is a temptation and therefore a sin. When Jesus repeatedly asked several of his disciples to come watch and pray with him in the garden of Gethsemane just before he was arrested, the reason he gave was, "Lest you fall into temptation." The temptation he was most concerned they would fall into was fear, which was exactly what they succumbed to. They became afraid when the centurions came to arrest

Jesus. When Jesus was taken away, all of his disciples quickly dispersed. And Peter, as Jesus foretold, denied him three times, and each time he did so out of fear.

The general trend for most local church congregations is that as they get bigger, individual giving will generally increase, resulting in the need for larger and larger church buildings. This is not always the case, though. The recent trend has been, in many cases, that rather than increasing the size of a physical structure, the number of worship services offered is increased. That way, congregations can remain intact without the church losing the income streams the congregations provide.

The other side of this is that there almost seems to be a cause-and-effect relationship between the increase in the size of congregations, the continued neglect of the widows and the fatherless, and an increase in crime and the need for either larger and/or more prisons. Increases in congregational numbers, leading to either larger buildings or an increase in the number of services, when our worship is considered by God to be "impure and defiled," though it may have the appearance of God's blessing with the outward appearances of success, the conditions of those living in the poorest urban neighborhoods surrounding us would indicate just the opposite.

As long as we are unwilling to admit that there just might be a cause-and-effect relationship between our impure and defiled worship and the increase in the number of violent crimes and of those incarcerated who grew up in single- or widowed-mother households, we will continue to point the finger of blame elsewhere. And that elsewhere always seems to be the political and civil authorities we accuse of trying to force down our throats legislation that goes against some of our strongest-held beliefs—with "visiting the widows and the fatherless in their distress" being, unfortunately, not one of them.

Finally, before ending this chapter, I make a final plea for widows. It is no secret that baby boomers represent the largest retirement demographic since Social Security was started. At some point, and statics point to age eighty-five, "only 13% of married women will still be living with their spouse."[38] This means that our churches will, in a few short years, be filled with the widows of all the baby boomer generation church leadership. Not to mention the widows of all other leadership (civil and political), both local and national. The present church leadership has not prepared future generations of leaders to ensure even the care of their own widowed wives once they leave them behind, never mind the present need to care for widows that already exists. This means that the number of older widows needing care will soon reach catastrophic proportions. And that does not even include all the younger widowed single moms that I believe have already reached catastrophic proportions.

The following is according to a report prepared by Anna M. Rappaport in October 2014:

- Women at age sixty-five are expected to live an average of twenty more years and men an average of eighteen more years. But women are also expected to have longer periods of disability in old age.
- Women work an average of twelve years less over their lifetimes due largely to caregiving responsibilities.
- Women earn less—women's earnings are 77 percent of men's earnings on average.
- Women are much less likely to remarry, but when men lose spouses, they are likely to remarry.
- Women often marry older spouses, leading to long periods of widowhood.
- Women's median retirement income is 58 percent of men's median retirement income due not only to increased rates of divorce but also to the expectation that divorce rates will continue to increase.
- Of women who are older and alone, 40 percent will have no other income source except Social Security.
- Women are much less likely to have a family caregiver available when they need help than men are, and women are also much

more likely to need paid help or be institutionalized than men are.

- Women, because they are the longer-lived person in a couple, are, when retirement resources are inadequate, the ones who are most likely to experience greater financial needs and problems.[39]

How can we truly expect there to be respect in this country for our beliefs concerning the sanctity of marriage when it is so apparent, based on our neglect of the widows and the fatherless, that in our relationship with Jesus as his betrothed, we have been living in an adulterous relationship with the world for far too long, so long, in fact, that it is doubtful our desolate condition either can, or will be, reversed?

Chapter 23: Worship Revisited

Since God said that Adam's purpose was "to dress and to keep the garden," it is clear that worship is God's primary directive for us in all things. When God divorces Adam and Eve because of their adulterous act of self-worship, this not only makes them the first condition of widowhood but their devotion to him on earth is also compromised thereafter. Thus, the need for a savior in the person of Jesus, who would also be bridegroom and husband, is vital—for through him the way that had been blocked for us to enter into paradise would once again be open. And although we will remain compromised in our devotion to God while we remain on earth, Jesus, by example, modeled for us God's standard in all things relating to worship.

Because our understanding of worship appears to be based almost solely on our worship-service-centered faith practices, and therefore, in my opinion, the single greatest root cause of deception in the church today; I also realize that there will no doubt be a great deal of resistance for recognizing and accepting this truth. I also fully recognize the fact that no matter how much scripturally based evidence is added to this supposition it probably will not sway those who are determined to resist the idea that the church could possibly be as far away from representing Jesus to the world as it has become.

Again, I am convinced that the greatest indication that our understanding of worship is an assumed understanding rather than an accurate one is the obvious neglect of the fatherless and the widows in their distress by churches that exists today. This is why the majority of *Spiritual Widowhood* has been focused on James 1:27 as the basis for proving how critical it is for our worship to be "pure and undefiled," and why.

Although a case has already been made for worship in chapters 9, 10, and 11 stemming from the establishment of a more accurate understanding of the word *religion* in James 1:27, the necessity for providing an even more compelling case, based on the ways that Jesus modeled worship for us, not only outside of the temple but also beyond the city gates of Jerusalem, remains, especially in light of the fact that there are few cases recorded of Jesus actually being in the temple, which, in and of itself, should speak volumes to us about the ways that Jesus, by his own words and actions, intended to draw us away from all of the deceptive influences relating to worship as being primarily identified with and carried out in a setting such as the one that both Jerusalem and the temple represented to the Jewish people.

For nearly two thousand years now, Paul has been telling God's people through Romans 12:1, "Therefore, I urge you, brethren, by the mercies of God, to present your bodies a living and holy sacrifice, acceptable to God, which is your spiritual service of worship" (NASB). Obviously, Jesus was the first "living and holy sacrifice, acceptable to God," and as such he serves as our only model for what "spiritual service of worship" looks like.

The Greek word for *worship* used in this passage is *latreia*.[40] If you will remember, in chapter 10 we learned the Hebrew word meaning "to dress it"—*'abad*[41]—which is akin to this Greek New Testament word *latreuo*, both of which mean "to serve, or service" in the context of worship.

What does it mean, though, "to present our bodies as a living and holy sacrifice, acceptable to God, which is our spiritual service of worship" (NASB)?" Something, admittedly, that comes across as being so abstract, which then only becomes that much more confounding when added to this the fact that most of our context for understanding worship today comes from a worship service, is it any wonder that we don't know how to apply this to our own lives any more than we know exactly what the last line of James 1:27—"to keep oneself unstained from the world"—means (NIV)?

I am convinced that what Paul is really saying to us in Romans 12:1 is to "love God with our hearts, minds and souls and to love our neighbors as ourselves," the fulfillment of which means that our bodies, as temples of the Lord, are being offered up as "living and holy sacrifices acceptable to God" (NASB) every moment of every day. And in two distinct instances, Jesus gives us a very clear picture of what this looks like, one of which he personally models for us and the other of which he presents through a parable.

The first example I am referring to is the account of the Samaritan woman whom Jesus personally met by a well on his way to Samaria from Galilee (John 4:3–43). The second example is the account of Jesus telling the parable of the Good Samaritan (Luke 10:25–37). Both are about worship, but neither seems to be understood in this context or serves to illustrate what being a "living and holy sacrifice acceptable to God" (NASB) should look like. It is supposed to look like Jesus, and the only way we can find out what Jesus looks like is to read Gospel accounts like these. In fact, I have come to believe, based on these two Gospel accounts alone, that the picture we have today of what being "living and holy sacrifices acceptable to God" (NASB) is supposed to look like doesn't resemble Jesus at all.

Chapter 24: The Samaritan Woman at the Well

There is so much for us to learn about worship in John's account of Jesus's encounter with the Samaritan woman he met at the well. Also worthy of note is the fact that this encounter has only been recorded in the Gospel of John, which actually may reveal much to us as to why John was referred to as the disciple whom Jesus loved. He seems to have had an understanding of his relationship with Jesus as the Messiah that none of the other disciples had. And just as Jesus entrusts John with his widowed mother as his last act on the cross, also only recorded in John's gospel account, it stands to reason that if any gospel account would include the encounter with the Samaritan woman, it would be John's, especially when considering the significance of this encounter and who the woman should be understood to represent here.

The first point made about this account is in John 4:4, where we learn that Jesus left Judea and was going to Galilee. This passage tells us that "he had to go through Samaria" to get there. This was the shortest route to take, but Jewish leaders would typically take a longer route in order to avoid the Samaritan people. The Jews had a long history of dislike for the Samaritans, so Jesus, not only choosing to take this route but also, according to verse 4, *having to take it*, should convict even the most complacent and fearful followers of Jesus that *we all have to go* to those places that represent to us what the Samaritans represented to the Jews.

It is critically important to remember not only that Jesus *had to go* but also who it was that sent him. It was his Father in heaven, and the reason we know this is that Jesus repeatedly tells us that everything he does is to fulfill his Father's will and not his own. The one time he was tempted not to, in the garden of Gethsemane before he was arrested, he quickly recanted: "Not my will but my father's will be done," which, again, is right out of the Lord's Prayer: "Thy will be done on earth as it is in heaven."

I wonder how often any or all of us are guilty of choosing to take the route that allows us to avoid having to come into contact with, or even to see, those whom we prefer not to see? It is no wonder that when Jesus arrives at the well and encounters the Samaritan woman, her response is one of confusion, and perhaps even disbelief. John 4:9 reads, "How is it you being a Jew ask me for a drink…? Jews have no dealings with Samaritans."

There is obviously much that Jesus could have said in response to these words expressed by this woman, but instead he gets right to the point. And he does so in a way that is completely relatable to her. She is there to get water, and he draws her into the message of salvation with a metaphor, telling her that if she had "living water" (verse 10), she would never thirst again. This "living water," she quickly concludes, will make her life easier, because if she has it she will never thirst again (verses 14–15), which would mean that she wouldn't have to go to the well and get water every day. It is also generally the case with all of us to first think of ways we can benefit, and our lives made easier, rather than using what we have or know to benefit others through the fulfillment of our Father's will.

Again, Jesus moves the conversation along, because he isn't finished with where he wants to go with it, and so he tells the woman to go and get her husband. When she tells him in response that she doesn't have a husband, Jesus reveals to her what he already knew before he asked her the question: that she doesn't have a husband. In fact, he knew, and he told her that she had five previous husbands and that the man she was presently living with, she wasn't even married to (verses 16–18).

By this time, Jesus really has the woman's attention, which is evidenced by the fact that she has quickly surmised that the only way he could know this about her is if he were a prophet. If we understand this encounter that Jesus had with the Samaritan woman, however, based on face value alone, then we will probably miss the larger context of who God intends for the woman to symbolize to us, thus making her realization that Jesus is a prophet far less profound than it actually was.

The Samaritan woman, and the fact that she had five husbands coupled with the fact that the man she was presently living with was not her husband, in the larger context of what Jesus is trying to get across to us, she could be said to symbolize the history of Israel's own relationship with God. How many times throughout Israel's history did God "divorce" Israel because of its adultery/idolatry? And what was it that Jesus said to the Pharisees in Matthew 23:38? "Behold, your house is left unto you desolate." As was pointed out in chapter 14, the word *desolate* used here means, "bereft," that is, "of a flock deserted by the shepherd or of a woman neglected by her husband, from who the husband withholds himself." [43]

Israel's heart has become so hard that not only do they not realize that God has left the building, but also they do not even recognize their rightful husband, Jesus, who is standing right in front of them outside the temple, and that they are once again guilty of living in an adulterous relationship with the world. What makes this encounter with the woman at the well equally profound is that her sin is not any worse or better than Israel's. The irony is that although she as a Samaritan was despised by the Jews, she nonetheless was quick to realize, first, that Jesus must be a prophet, and second, even more profoundly, that he was the promised Messiah, whereas those who should have immediately grasped this had become so deceived as to themselves becoming the deceivers of others, that they either could not, or would not, recognize who Jesus really was.

In verse 20, following the Samaritan's discovery that Jesus "must be a prophet," she, not Jesus, then brings up the subject of worship. There is only one other instance where worship comes up this early in the Gospel accounts, and that is when Satan tries to tempt Jesus in Matthew 4:10, which reads, "Jesus said to him, "Away from me, Satan!

For it is written: 'Worship the Lord your God, and serve him only" (NIV). In this case, the word *worship* used here is from the Greek word *proskyneō*,[44] which is most commonly translated as *worship*. The word *serve*, however, at the end of this verse, is the Greek word *latreuo*, which, it should be remembered, is the same word used to mean "spiritual service of worship" (NASB) in Romans 12:1 (see previous chapter) and is similar in meaning, if you will remember, to the Hebrew word translated as "to dress it" in Genesis 2:15 (covered in chapter 10, as well as chapter 23).[45]

Other than this instance, there is no other time that the subject of worship comes up this early in the Gospel accounts, especially in this context. As was mentioned in the previous paragraph, it was the Samaritan woman who first mentioned worship. Based on her comments in verse 20, it seems apparent that she is still trying to make sense of everything that is going on here and why this Jew, whom she has now come to believe is a prophet, is having this conversation with her. "Our fathers," she tells him, "worshipped in this mountain; and you say, that in Jerusalem is the place where men ought to worship." This might be the equivalent today of saying, "If you really want to worship God, you have to come to our church, or a church in our denomination."

Jesus's response to her, though, is profound, so profound in fact that we still do not seem to have grasped what he really meant by what he said. He tells the Samaritan woman in verse 21 that worship, essentially, will not be associated with a specific time or place. He is saying, in effect, that no one will be able to make the claim of having the exclusive right of worshipping God based on location, time, style of worship, etc.

Also, if there was any doubt about who this Samaritan woman symbolizes for us, Jesus clearly establishes this when he addresses her in this same verse as "woman." Obviously, Jesus does not intend for his address of her as "woman" to be confused with all of the significance being attached to his mother, Mary, when he addresses her in this same way, yet in terms of what Jesus says to the Samaritan woman following this about worship, it would be too much of a coincidence if Jesus's encounter with her, this early in John's gospel account, was anything but an opportunity to dispel the ways that worship had become associated with a building and defined through worship-service-centered faith practices.

Jesus then goes on to say in verse 22 that it doesn't matter where you are worshipping as long as you know the truth of salvation, as the playing field is about to become level, which idea is clearly presented in Ephesians 2, the entire chapter. Ephesians 2 makes it clear that God has, through Jesus, removed the dividing wall between Jews and Gentiles. Ephesians 2:19 reads, "Now therefore you are no more strangers and foreigners, but fellow citizens with the saints, and of the household of God," which, incidentally, would explain why only "the fatherless and the widows" are included in James 1:27, because now there is no such thing as a "stranger, or a foreigner" when it comes to the people whom God considers to be his chosen people. His chosen people are those whom he has chosen and who have accepted his Son's proposal of marriage.

This is confirmed in Romans 2:28–29: "For he is not a Jew, which is one outwardly, neither is that circumcision, which is outward in the flesh: But he is a Jew, which is one inwardly; and circumcision is that of the heart, in the Spirit, and not in the letter: whose praise is not of men, but of God" (KJV).

If you are thinking at this point that a lot is being read into Jesus's encounter with the Samaritan woman, John 4:23–24 will hopefully leave little room for doubt—if we can only understand and accept it, that is, in the context of what worship is supposed to look like, with Jesus being our model for what it means to be "a living and holy sacrifice." "Yet a time is coming and has now come when the true worshipers will worship the Father in the Spirit and in truth, for they are the kind of worshipers the Father seeks. God is spirit, and his worshipers must worship in the Spirit and in truth" (NIV).

Jesus does not just say that "the hour cometh"; he also says that it is already here, the reason being that he was there, not just there as in here on earth, but literally there at that moment in time speaking with the Samaritan woman on his way to Galilee. And he had just told her this in response to her statement about worship, that "our fathers worshipped on this mountain," whereas the Jews maintained that in order to really worship God, you had to go to Jerusalem.

Jesus is literally telling the Samaritan woman, and subsequently all of us today who claim Jesus as our betrothed, that his encounter with her is a picture of the kind of worshippers God wants us to be. Jesus is modeling for us what worshipping God "in spirit and in truth" looks like, and it doesn't look anything like the way we have come to define worship strictly based on our worship-service-centered faith practices.

In fact, I don't know how many times I have heard over the years in a church "worship service" setting verse 24 quoted: that God wants us to worship him in spirit and in truth. And what follows during the course of the "worship-led" service is supposed to fulfill what Jesus meant when he said this to the Samaritan woman—which is really hard to understand, since they were obviously not anywhere near a physical church building, much less in a worship service. No, what Jesus is presenting to us through his encounter with the Samaritan woman, as the "first living and holy sacrifice," is a picture of what the service of worship "in spirit and in truth" looks like.

The Greek word for *worshippers* in verse 23, when Jesus tells the Samaritan woman "the true worshippers shall worship the Father in spirit and in truth," is *proskynētēs*.[46] This Greek word is only used this one time in the New Testament. Jesus is speaking of how radically different those who will accept his proposal of marriage, going forward, are to fulfill what it means to worship God in spirit and in truth through the service of worship, especially outside the church walls, which is exactly what we are told in Hebrews 13:12–14: "Therefore Jesus also, that he might sanctify the people through His own blood, suffered outside the gate. So, let us go out to Him outside the camp, bearing His reproach. For here we do not have a lasting city, but we are seeking the city which is to come" (NASB).

Immediately following this, in Hebrews 13:15–16, we learn, "Through him then, let us continually offer up a sacrifice of praise to God, that is, the fruit of lips that give thanks to His name. And do not neglect doing good and sharing, for with such sacrifices God is pleased" (NASB). If the phrase "good works, deeds, or offerings" were used instead of the word *sacrifice*, then what is being said here might be understood for its intended significance. Both areas of sacrifice in this passage, though, fulfill the two greatest commandments: love God with your heart, mind, and soul, and love your neighbor as yourself.

It is no coincidence that this entire exhortation for us to come outside the city gates and bear Christ's reproach, along with the naming of the categories of "sacrifices that pleases God," comes fairly soon after Hebrews 13:4, which reads, "Marriage is to be held in honor among all, and the marriage bed is to be *undefiled*: but fornicators and adulterers God will judge" (NASB), which was previously discussed in chapter 11 as it relates to us as Christ's bride and to worship.

There are two verses in the New Testament that specifically mandate the giving of thanks to God in all things. The first one is Ephesians 5:20: "Giving thanks always for all things unto God and the Father in the name of our Lord Jesus Christ." The second one is found in 1 Thessalonians 5:18: "In everything give thanks: for this is the will of God in Christ Jesus concerning you."

The offering of thanks not only was but also remains a significant part of the sacrificial system for us today. One "rabbinical tradition teaches that all the Mosaic sacrifices would have an end except the thank offering, and all prayers would cease except the *prayer of thanksgiving*."[47]

Just to put the significance of the *thank offering* into perspective, the following are several examples where it is being offered up to God in both the Old Testament and New Testament, including the subsequent outcomes. From the Old Testament, the first one is in Daniel 6:10. After King Darius signed a decree stating that it was punishable by death to bow down to any other god except himself for thirty days, Daniel disobeyed the King's decree and continued to bow down to God and to face Jerusalem (east) three times a day, offering up prayer and "giving thanks." And we know, of course, that when Daniel was thrown into the lions' den as a consequence of disobeying King Darius's decree, God delivered him from being devoured by the lions.

The next instance from the Old Testament occurs in Jonah 2:9. Preceding this, God has instructed Jonah to go to Nineveh to cry out against the people there for their wickedness, but Jonah tries to flee and ends up getting thrown into the sea, where "he is swallowed by a great fish, in the belly of which he remained for three days and nights." It is only after being inside the fish for three days that Jonah finally cries out to God through prayer, which begins with verse 2:1 and ends with verse 2:9, when Jonah says, "But I will sacrifice to You with the voice of thanksgiving. That which I have vowed I will pay. Salvation is from the Lord" (NASB) Immediately following this, not unlike with Daniel's continued offering up of prayer and giving of thanks, God delivers Jonah from the belly of the fish. Verse 2:10 reads, "And the Lord spake unto the fish, and it vomited out Jonah upon the dry land."

Then in the New Testament, there are three instances involving Jesus giving thanks as "the first living and holy sacrifice" (NASB), and as our model for worship in all things. The first one is in Matthew 15:36, "when Jesus took seven loaves and the fishes, *gave thanks*, broke them, and gave them to his disciples, after which the disciples gave them to the multitude." Most of us are all too familiar with this passage and the miracle that followed. Four thousand men, plus women and children, were fed from these seven loaves and the fishes. Most of us probably think this is the basis for our own giving of thanks, or saying a blessing, before we eat a meal. Obviously, if Jesus said the blessing before feeding the multitudes, so should we. So, not giving thanks before eating a meal today is nearly paramount to a denial of our faith in Jesus. Yet, Jesus's act of *giving thanks* was (1) in accordance with God's will and (2) for the benefit of others over himself. It is literally, in this context of feeding the multitudes, fulfilling what it means to love God with our hearts, minds, and souls and also to love our neighbors as ourselves.

The next instance where Jesus gives thanks is in John 11:41–42, in a situation that does not even remotely have anything to do with food or a meal. It occurred when Lazarus was raised from the dead. "…Then Jesus looked up and said, 'Father, I thank you that you have heard me. I knew that you always hear me, but I said this for the benefit of the people standing here, that they may believe that you sent me" (NIV).

All of the people who were gathered outside of Lazarus's tomb and mourning his death were most likely Jews. When Jesus *gave thanks* out loud within earshot of the people around him so that they might believe that he was the Son of God, it was so that they would all know that he was giving a *thank offering*, a significant part of the sacrificial system. And the outcome, Lazarus being raised from the dead, was just like the ones recorded in Daniel and Jonah, and with Jesus feeding the multitudes: a miracle. And also in this case, as well as the cases involving Daniel and Jonah, it foreshadowed Jesus's own deliverance from death when he was resurrected on the third day after being crucified.

The final instance of the thank offering being offered up by Jesus is in the upper room when Jesus serves his disciples the Passover meal. Luke 22:17 reads, "And Jesus took the cup, and *gave thanks*, and said, Take this, and divide it among yourselves." Verse 19 tells us, "And he [Jesus] took the bread, and *gave thanks*, and brake it, and gave unto them."

Of course, there is a lot going on here, and much of it was covered in chapter 16, but the significance of the *thank offering* was not covered there. The Greek word for *gave thanks* is *eucharisteo*, a verb, and it simply means, "to be grateful, feel thankful, *give thanks*."[48] Whereas many Protestants use the term *Communion* to describe the sacrament of celebrating the Lord's Supper, the Anglican Church uses the term *Eucharist*. As you might imagine, this difference in terminology has a lot of history behind it, but most Christians probably would not have any sense of what those disputes were or even why different terminology is used.

What is significant about the term *Eucharist* is that it communicates the significance of the giving of thanks, which is something that we seem to have completely lost sight of, as well as all understanding for, today. If we don't take into account both the necessity and the significance of the *thank offering*, as well as *deed offerings* to be carried out by us, the church, as Jesus's betrothed, then we have truly lost sight of Jesus's own life example of what God requires from us when it comes to what he considers to be worship, especially for those acts of worship that he considers "pure and undefiled."

Although it may seem like I have veered off topic, or at least taken a detour, this discussion about word and deed sacrifices is more like a bend in the road where you lose sight of the horizon for just a moment, but the road and the direction you are traveling is the same. It is important to this discussion to always connect dots that may not have been connected before in order to present as clear a picture as possible of what God considers to be necessities in our daily worship of him.

Anything less than what God desires from the "true worshippers who will worship him in spirit and in truth" is a strong indication that deception has been allowed to creep in, with the strong possibly of its having completely overtaken us, resulting in what we consider to be houses of worship, from God's perspective, as now being nothing more than "dens of thieves."

And whenever this becomes the case, such a system, by perceived necessity, will be driven by the overpowering need for self-preservation, which will almost always include self-replication as the justified means for survival. It is ironic that we would condemn individuals for living out their lives in this way, which is what those who were giving out of their surplus in Mark 12:44 were doing, but when the church does it, it is for God and is therefore justified.

To put it another way, whenever it becomes the case that a church's or denomination's overriding drive becomes that of self-preservation and self-replication, that which is thought to be offered up to God with no benefit to the persons making the offerings, actually ends up being offered up to a system that only portrays itself as being one and the same with God, but in reality nothing could be further from the truth. That is to say, there arises the belief that the church system we are a part of is an accurate representation of God, and therefore giving to this system is the same as giving unto God. The paradox becomes, though, that the ones who are giving these offerings, being convinced that it brings no personal benefit or glory to self, but solely benefits what we have come to believe are firmly established, Biblically based, kingdom agendas, will actually end up being the chief recipients of his or her own offerings, along with everyone else. The system is one that not only is potentially stealing from God but also causing all who are a part of it to inadvertently steal what is meant only for God. That being the case, is it any wonder why Jesus turned over the tables in the temple?

Just as an aside, before Jesus turned over the tables, John tells us in chapter 2, verse 15, that Jesus first "made a scourge of cords and drove them all out of the temple, with the sheep and the oxen." After Jesus was arrested, "Pilate had him scourged before handing him over to be crucified" (Mark 15:15). That is to say, Jesus, who went into the temple and made a whip to use to drive out the animals along with the money changers before turning over the tables, would later, as the true temple of God, be scourged himself.

Returning to Jesus's encounter with the Samaritan woman by the well, after she has realized that he is not only a prophet but also the promised Messiah, apparently she becomes so excited that she forgets what she came there for: to draw water to take back with her. John 4:28 reads, "The woman then left her water pot, and went her way into the city, and said to the men, Come, see a man, which told me all things that ever I did: is not this the Christ?"

It is easy to imagine this to be an abbreviated account of what the Samaritan woman probably said to the men of the city. This is pure speculation on my part, but I don't think my idea is far-fetched. This woman has essentially become an evangelist, as most of us would agree that a significant part of evangelism is personal testimony. Most of us have probably heard enough personal testimonies, or given them ourselves, to know that what will typically be included is what we were like before accepting Jesus and what we became like afterward. Based on this, I can well imagine what else the Samaritan woman might have said about her encounter with Jesus. For instance, "He is a Jew, yet he didn't seem to mind that I was a Samaritan, or anything else he already knew about me. He seemed to accept me despite all these things." So, the Samaritan woman's response wasn't just based solely on Jesus's knowing and telling her about things he could not have possibly known; it was also everything else mixed in with it, especially the fact that he did not condemn her but instead conveyed God's love, respect, compassion, and mercy towards her.

It is also important to remember that the men the Samaritan woman encountered when she returned to her city and began to proselytize them also, in all likelihood, knew the same things that Jesus knew about her. Just the fact that a Jewish man had come to Samaria in the first place, I imagine, was fairly astonishing, but then knowing that this same Jewish man also knew what they knew about this woman, and yet still told her the way of salvation, was probably hard for them to digest. That Jesus had not condemned her, a sign that he obviously cared about her, could not have been lost on them.

Even today, our perceptions of this woman, just based on the fact that she had been married so many times and was presently living with a man, immediately calls to mind a scenario that most likely includes that she came from a dysfunctional family, was possibly raised in a single-parent home, and was probably the victim of either physical or sexual abuse (or both) growing up, obviously all of which resulted in an overall poor self-image, leading her to perpetually look for love everywhere but in the right places (and for the right reasons).

Yet Jesus, just by being there, demonstrated his desire to accept her just the way she was. And imagine how she must have felt when she found out that Jesus already knew what her life had been like up to that point but had shared his message of salvation with her like it didn't matter, because it didn't. Who better to go before him to those in the city he was traveling to proclaiming his imminent arrival? Imagine what his reception might have been like if she hadn't.

The outcomes going forward after Jesus's encounter with the Samaritan woman are not unlike those reported in Acts 6:7 after the Greek widows are fed. Jesus is so well received in the Samaritan woman's city that he is asked not to rush off. He remains with them for two days (verse 40). What everyone who has accepted Jesus's proposal of marriage comes to realize is exactly what is recorded in John 4:42: "Now we believe, not because of thy [the Samaritan woman's] saying: for we have heard him ourselves, and know that this is indeed the Christ, the Saviour of the world."

Isn't that what each of us can say about our betrothal experience, that first we heard the testimony of someone who had already accepted Jesus, and then our belief in their testimony was made real when Jesus came to visit us personally—and he has remained with us from that moment forward?

Understanding what God desires/requires from us in our worship of him is something that seems to be the greatest struggle, first with the Jews and now with all of us who claim betrothal to Jesus. Every time we lose sight of what Jesus has modeled for us through both word (the giving of thanks) and deed (loving our neighbors) is an indication that we have been deceived. And the measure of that deception, again, can always be determined by whether or not our worship can be described in the way that God has described it through James, as being "pure and undefiled."

Chapter 25: Jerusalem to Jericho

The second example for being a "living and holy sacrifice" to be discussed in the context of "worshipping God in spirit and in truth" is the parable of the Good Samaritan found in Luke 10:25–37. This parable, told by Jesus, is in response to the question put to him by an interpreter of the law, "And who is my neighbor?"

Although not typically interpreted in this way, what Jesus is ultimately providing us with is a picture of worship, one that reveals Israel's own present condition of desolation based on her worship practices; what Jesus has come to fulfill through the offering of his own life as the ultimate loving act of worship; and what worship must include going forward "…when the true worshipers will worship the Father in the Spirit and in truth, for they are the kind of worshipers the Father seeks. God is spirit, and his worshipers must worship in the Spirit and in truth" (NIV).

Not surprisingly, like Jesus's encounter with the Samaritan woman at the well, the setting for this parable, along the Jericho road, is outside of Jerusalem, with some evidence even suggesting that the Jericho road left the city from the Sheeps' gate. This cannot be conclusively proven, but based on an interpretation of this parable in the context of worship, it would certainly be consistent with the overall message Jesus presents.

Many of us probably first heard this parable as children, which was my personal experience. It was during vacation Bible school when I was about six years old (1962). The older kids put on a puppet show for the younger kids using puppets they made out of bendable pipe cleaners. On a very basic level, the message that anyone, regardless of age, takes away from this is the golden rule: "Do unto others as you would have them do unto you" (Matthew 7:12).

The Samaritan in this parable is obviously the hero, and most of us, as children, want to be heroes; thus, the emphasis is always placed on being like the Samaritan. And since there is little dispute that Jesus has put himself in this parable as the Samaritan, this ultimately means being like Jesus. Perhaps the irony is that for the majority culture in Israel, the last thing they aspired to be like was someone of this minority culture. This distinction was certainly not emphasized to me in church as a child growing up in the South during the time of segregation and the civil rights movement.

The question asked by the interpreter of the law, "And who is my neighbor?," which prompted Jesus to tell this parable in the first place, was actually the second question asked by this same lawyer. The first question he asked Jesus was, "Master, what shall I do to inherit eternal life?" Jesus, knowing that the lawyer was trying to test him, answered with his own question, "What is written in the law?" He replied. "How do you read it" (NIV)?

How many of us are guilty, and I include myself, of asking someone a theological question when we already know the answer? This lawyer, obviously, wants Jesus, as well as everyone else listening, to know that he knows the right answer, and also perhaps to prove to everyone that either Jesus doesn't know it or that Jesus isn't any more of an authority on the law than he is. Jesus knows the lawyer's heart, though, and is not about to be used to make the lawyer appear to be more than he is. Ironically, if the lawyer had been as secure in his own faith identity as he was trying to appear to be, he probably wouldn't have had the need to test Jesus in the first place.

The lawyer, of course, well versed in the law, answers Jesus's question with a precise and scripturally correct answer: "Thou shalt love the Lord thy God with all thy heart, and with all thy soul, and with all thy strength, and with all thy mind [which is the picture of "a living and holy sacrifice, holy and acceptable to God]; and thy neighbor as thyself [fulfilled as our spiritual service of worship]."

Jesus graciously affirms that this lawyer's answer is correct, saying,

"Thou has answered right: do this, and thou shalt live." It would seem, though, that Jesus's affirmation only stirred the lawyer's need for more of the same. Paradoxically, whereas the lawyer set out to lay a trap for Jesus, he unknowingly ensnares himself with his next question, which appears in Luke 10:29: "But he, willing to justify himself, said unto Jesus, And who is my neighbor" (KJV)?

The Greek word for *justify* used here is *dikaioō*, and it basically means that the lawyer wanted to be "rendered, or considered to be righteous."[49] As part of the majority culture, as well as having a position of authority in that culture, the lawyer may well have believed that both of these facts were more than sufficient proof to establish that he was living a righteous life in God's eyes. He may have also thought that because Jesus had affirmed him as having answered correctly when asked what was required to inherit eternal life, and based on whom he perceived his neighbors to be, that Jesus would prove him to be the righteous person he already considered himself to be.

Which brings us to the second similarity between the parable Jesus told in response to the lawyer's second question and the account of Jesus's encounter with the woman at the well. In both instances, the central figure is a Samaritan. And based on whom the lawyer probably considered his neighbors to be, likely those who were demographically most similar to him and who could easily return any favor they received from him, he probably felt that he had more than abundantly loved these neighbors as himself.

Jesus, without missing a beat, though, launches into the following parable, which begins in verse 30:

> A certain man went down from Jerusalem to Jericho, and fell among thieves, which stripped him of his raiment (clothes), and wounded him, and departed, leaving him half dead. And by chance there came down a certain priest that way: and when he saw him, he passed by on the other side. And likewise a Levite, when he was at the place, came and looked on him, and passed by on the other side. But a certain Samaritan,

> as he journeyed, came where he was: and when he saw
> him, he had compassion on him. (KJV)

In just four verses, Jesus manages to get all up in the lawyer's face. Perhaps the lawyer, because he is still expecting this to put him in a positive light, does not catch on right away. Or maybe he realizes as soon as Jesus says this that his plan has backfired. Either way, at this point, he probably has no choice but to just wait Jesus out.

Because Jesus includes a Samaritan in this parable and tells the lawyer that it was this man, and not the priest or the Levite, who had compassion on the victim, the lawyer, one might imagine, probably perceived it as being as offensive as a slap in the face with a pork chop. Because this lawyer is very well versed in the law, though, he might have thought that the priest and the Levite were justified in passing the victim by, as he himself might well have done. The victim had been stripped of his clothes, so there was probably no way to determine his station in life (his clothing would have indicated that) or, perhaps, even his ethnicity.

The fact that the man was half dead, which also meant that he was half alive, didn't really matter. He probably looked dead, but even if he wasn't dead, he might have been too far gone to risk helping. And besides, what if he wasn't a Jew? What if he was a Gentile, or a Samaritan? Even if he weren't dead, he would have still been considered to be unclean. Whether he was dead or was going to die shortly after, according to Numbers 19:11–22, coming into contact with someone who is dead makes you unclean for seven days—an inconvenience the priest and the Levite apparently were not willing to risk.

On the other hand, the lawyer might have thought that the Samaritan stopping to help was no big deal, because he had nothing to lose. But this should have also been the attitude of the priest and the Levite. Their faith in God, just as our faith in Jesus, truly means we have nothing to lose. The only thing that was probably certain in the lawyer's mind at that point was that the Samaritan represented someone whom a Jewish leader like him knew to avoid, which was already pointed out in chapter 24 when discussing the significance of

Jesus's having to go to Samaria on his way to Galilee. Jews, especially if they were leaders of the faith, typically avoided taking that route, even though it was shorter, just to avoid seeing or having any contact with the Samaritans, which is not so different from the attitudes and actions today when it comes to majority culture and their avoidance of minority cultures.

What is most interesting about all three of these figures that Jesus put into this parable is that as each one comes upon the victim, all three look at him (the same Greek word translated as "saw" in verses 31 and 33 and as "looked" in verse 32), which is what we all probably would have done, because that's what we do. Our brains immediately begin to process massive amounts of information, including what the right thing to do is, battling it out with as many justifications we can come up with for not doing what is right. Most of those justifications, though, have as their basis fear and selfishness, neither of which stems from love. Fear of the Lord is quickly overridden by fear for self, especially in the areas of personal financial loss and/or loss of time, being late to fulfill our high calling so to speak, and/or suffering bodily harm.

One, or all three, of these factors might have been the priest's and the Levite's justification for passing by the victim on the other side of the road, but who among us can condemn them for this, in that all of us have probably been guilty of the same? Notice that Jesus does not condemn them for their actions, but he doesn't praise them, either. Jesus's point is much greater than this. He is trying to illustrate the condition of the Jewish leadership, and thus the religious system as a whole, based entirely on what God considers worship to be.

And whether the lawyer realizes this or not, this point being made by Jesus is literally connected to the basis for what he told the Pharisees in Matthew 23:38: "Behold your house has been left unto you desolate," which brings us to the need to understand who Jesus intends for the victim in this account to represent. Perhaps it is obvious, but in case it isn't, the victim represents us, the church, the bride that Jesus came to deliver, redeem and restore (the "victim" also represents Jesus as well, but this will be discussed in more detail later in the chapter), both as a result of the heavy yoke that the Jewish leaders had placed upon those entrusted to their care, as well as those who were not Jewish by birth. Which, ironically, would also make the priest and the Levite to be like the victim on the side of the road the condition of being half dead because of their own denial of Jesus. This would apply as well to all who are not physically dead, but who are also not yet in the household of faith for being likened to what might be accurately characterized today as zombies—the physically walking/living, but who are spiritually dead.

Matthew 23:13-15 reads as follows:

> Woe to you teachers of the law and Pharisees, you hypocrites! You shut the door of the kingdom of heaven in people's faces. You yourselves do not enter, nor will you let those enter who are trying to. Woe to you, teachers of the law and Pharisees, you hypocrites! You travel over land and sea to win a single convert, and when you have succeeded, you make them twice as much a child of hell as you are. (NIV)

Matthew 23:3–6, which precedes the above section of this chapter, is yet another section of scripture reinforcing not only the passages in the previous paragraph but also what Jesus is really trying to get across in this parable. In verse 3, he point-blank tells the religious leaders that those under their care "…must be careful to do everything they tell them. But should not do what you do, for you do not practice what you preach (NIV)." Then in the next verse, Jesus puts it to them even more harshly by saying that "you place many demands upon those in your care, essentially to conform to your system (a system rooted in deception), the subsequent weight of which is placed on the people's shoulders, and yet you as leaders won't even lift a finger to help those in your care to move it along" (no doubt where the saying comes from "won't lift a finger to help).

Matthew 11:28–30 reads, "Come to me, all you who are weary and burdened, and I will give you rest. Take my yoke upon you and learn from me, for I am gentle and humble in heart, and you will find rest for your souls. For my yoke is easy and my burden is light" (NIV). When we understand that the victim in this parable represents the church that Jesus came to redeem, thus taking on our own yoke that is crushing us under its weight in exchange for his, we can then easily realize that the priest, the Levite, and the thieves who attacked the victim and left him half dead by the side of the road are one and the same. Jesus is literally telling the lawyer that the priest and the Levite represent him (the lawyer), as well as all the other religious leaders, and that what they are guilty of doing to those under their care is no different from what the thieves did to this victim. They are exactly the same in God's eyes.

This also becomes a prime example of what Jesus said to the Pharisees in Matthew 23:3, which has been previously mentioned: "So you must be careful to do everything they tell you. But do not do what they do, for they do not practice what they preach" (NIV). It is also consistent with what Jesus said in Mark 11:17, when he went into the temple, herded the animals out, and overturned the money changers' tables: "Is it not written, My house shall be called of all nations the house of prayer? But you have made it a den of thieves." What is most interesting of all is that the religious leaders do not dispute Jesus but instead fear him (a fear, unfortunately, that does not lead to wisdom). Verse 18 of this same chapter reads, "And the scribes and chief priests heard it, and sought how they might destroy him: for they feared him, because all the people were astonished at his doctrine." Obviously, "the fear of the Lord is the beginning of wisdom" was not the case when it came to anything Jesus said and did.

It is worth noting again that the opposite of wisdom is foolishness (first noted on page 28). And again, if the fear of God is the beginning of wisdom, then the fear of humankind is foolishness. Since the religious leaders did not recognize Jesus as God but just as a man, their fear is consistent with what the fear of humankind leads to: foolishness.

If we do not think that this could be us today because we know and teach the truth of salvation based on acceptance of Jesus and we believe that what was going on in Israel was salvation based on works, it is time for us to reevaluate.

According to 2 Corinthians 11:4, "For if someone comes to you and preaches a Jesus, other than the Jesus we preached, or if ye receive a different spirit from the Spirit you received, or a different gospel from the one you accepted, you put up with it easily enough" (NIV). Based on this passage, it is possible to have the right Jesus for salvation and the wrong Jesus for living it out. And living it out has to be based on God's worship standards for what it means to love him with our entire being and to love our neighbors as ourselves.

The lawyer in this parable knew the truth of salvation. One did not receive it based on works; it was based on living salvation out through works (word/deed offerings). This is also true for us in Christ. But what we have come to think of as works are considered by God to be offerings. If we go out and lead someone to Christ and then tell that person that he or she must conform to our prescribed system as the only pure system for living out an uncompromised life of faith, don't we just end up leading that person away from Christ? Isn't that essentially what Jesus was telling the Pharisees in Matthew 23:15, when he said to them that the converts they made "became twice as much a child of hell as they were?"

Although, it might be really difficult to get our minds around this, have we not become guilty of the same? As soon as someone is "saved," we start telling them that in order to be conformed to the image of Jesus, they need to start having quiet time every morning, pray a certain amount of time each day, join a church, give at least 10 percent of their income to the church, join a Sunday school class and/or a small group in the church, and that the Christians who most love the Lord will be in church at all the appropriate times for all of the appropriate worship opportunities. Also, there is to be no drinking, no smoking, no R-rated movies, no, no, no, no, no, no! Essentially, fulfilling "the list," has become in our minds what it means to be holy.

And this is just the short list. A whole book could be written about the system of works that we have come to believe is what illustrates whether or not we have been conformed to the image of Christ. Obviously, since we know and teach the truth of salvation, everything else must also be correct, right? And therefore there is no way that we could have possibly arrived at the place where our leaders are just as guilty today of deceiving those entrusted to their care as the leaders whom Jesus confronted were—and for the exact same reasons; impossible, right?

And yet Jesus's own example as the first "living and holy sacrifice," and his modeling of what our "spiritual service of worship" should look like in order to resemble him, are both based on his encounter with the Samaritan woman at the well and the parable of the Good Samaritan, which present this truth without blemish and with absolute clarity.

If you are still not convinced, then consider yet another instance in Matthew 15:7–9, where Jesus, once again, is telling a group of "Pharisees and interpreters of the law who had come to confront him for breaking the traditions of the elders. "... You hypocrites, rightly did Isaiah prophesy of you: "This people honors me with their lips, but their heart is far away from me. But in vain do they worship me, teaching as doctrines the precepts of men" (NASB). And these words he spoke are almost a direct quote from Isaiah 29:13: "Wherefore the Lord said, Forasmuch as this people draw near me with their mouth, and with their lips do honor me, but have removed their heart far from me, and their fear toward me is taught by the precept of men" (KJV).

God has always, and will always, base the nearness of our heart on our capacity for acts of mercy and compassion. We are all so vulnerable to being deceived into believing that any time we gather together to worship God through praise and song, that it is automatically an indication of the nearness of our hearts to God.

In James 4:8, we are told to "Draw near to God and he will draw near to you. Cleanse your hands, you sinners; and purify your hearts, you double-minded" (NIV). What we may have failed to realize is how James means for us to "draw near to God, having more to do with loving our neighbors as ourselves than how many worship services we attend, or how much time we spend in scripture, or how long we pray each day.

Which has been made more than abundantly clear in Matthew 25:31–46, when Jesus is on his throne and all the nations are gathered before him, and after telling us that he will separate the people in the same way that a shepherd separates the sheep from the goats, in verse

40 he reveals what his criteria will be based on for separating the people, "whatever you did for one of the least of these brothers and sister of mine, you did for me" (NIV). Raising the question: *How can we possibly draw near to God, and He to us, when we keep those who are dear to Him at arm's length?* Drawing near, for instance, to the victim lying by the side of the road in this parable, whom the priest and the Levite pass by.

What is particularly significant about Jesus's criteria for separating the sheep and the goats is the use of the very personal "*you.*" He says that "*you* have done this to the very least of these," not that you have only paid someone else to do unto the very least of these, or that only your church has done unto the very least of these. He doesn't even say that because you are a member of a church and pay your tithe, this qualifies you for having done this in God's eyes. This point is especially being made in this parable by the fact that Jesus has individuals going down this road and passing by on the other side, regardless of the fact that they represent a larger corporate body. At the same time, because they are part of the Jewish leadership, they equally reflect the condition of their respective corporate bodies, the condition of which is largely due to their own influence. The unalterable bottom line is that each of us, individually, is responsible for serving the least of these, and for the same reason that Jesus came: to serve and not be served.

A good illustration for this is found during the time of the Civil War in this country. Men in the North who were wealthy enough could avoid being drafted by paying someone else to serve in the war in their place. In other words, they opted out of front-line duty. Our wealth, our status in society, or our office in the church does not exempt us from front-line duty. In fact, those who have been given much, including positions of church leadership, have the added burden of being those who have the greatest responsibility for leading those entrusting themselves to their care, outside of the church doors—and onto the frontlines.

One of the best examples I have personally ever witnessed this take place in the context of local church leadership was modeled by a youth pastor who came to me a number of years ago and asked about volunteering with us serving widows. His name is Aaron Tolson, and he is the assistant pastor of high school youth at Lookout Mountain Presbyterian Church. Soon after our meeting, Aaron started coming down once a week and served with Dick Mason, Widows Harvest Ministries' then coordinator for home repair projects for widows. After Aaron had worked with Dick on a number of home repair projects on widows' homes, he began to invite some of his youth to join him. Now, many years later, his youth come out and serve one Saturday a month during the school year and almost every Saturday during the summer. Additionally, they spend a week with us each summer participating in a short-term mission opportunity we host. This is the closest thing I have ever seen for what I am convinced was Jesus's own model of discipleship of the service of worship. And as you might have already suspected, Aaron, like Alfred Johnson, has also become another one of my personal heroes.

After Jesus has finished setting the stage for the parable of the Good Samaritan, including having named most of its characters, he introduces the Samaritan. So from that point forward there is a shift from Jesus presenting the symptoms that he has diagnosed based on his assessment of the desolate condition of Israel's house to not only what he has come to do but also what worship in spirit and truth must look like going forward if we are to look, act, and—most importantly—be like him.

As soon as Jesus tells the lawyer that the Samaritan was the only one of the three to be moved with compassion when he saw the victim, it is doubtful that the lawyer understood that the Samaritan was supposed to represent Jesus. If he had understood, then words like *blasphemy* might have come to his mind. Probably the only thing still on the lawyer's mind was the slap-in-the-face-with-a-pork-chop, Samaritan-as-righteous-hero insult.

It seems pretty obvious, at least based on the information we are given up to this point that the lawyer doesn't recognize, or at least concede, that Jesus is the Son of God. So how could he have any idea what the bigger picture was that Jesus was trying to present, a picture that even today those who are betrothed to Jesus seem to have a hard time understanding? What a stark contrast this is, though, between the Samaritan woman at the well who comes to recognize and accept Jesus as the promised Messiah and this lawyer who has tried to set a trap for Jesus.

Remembering the Samaritan's reaction when he comes upon the victim, namely, that "he has compassion on him," not only reminds us of John 3:16 (seeing as God, being moved with compassion for us, sent his only begotten Son) but also paints a picture of the compassion Jesus exhibits in John 11:35. Right before Jesus raised Lazarus from the dead, when Mary and all of those who were with her came to him weeping, scripture records that "Jesus wept."

For anyone not familiar with Jewish traditions, when a Jewish person dies, mourners come and sit with the family for seven days. This practice is called "sitting shivah" (*shivah* means "seven").[50] Those Jews who were mourning and weeping with Mary were no doubt sitting shivah. What is most interesting, as well as revealing, about what is taking place here is that the Greek word translated as the word for weeping to describe Mary's and the mourners' weeping, which is klaiō, is a different word from the one used in the translation "Jesus wept," which is dakyrō.

The first word, klaiō, is a verb and "describes the weeping over the dead, a mournful weep."[51] The word used in "Jesus wept," dakyrō, is also a verb, but it just simply means "to weep, shed tears."[52] Jesus is literally weeping, dakyrō, with the mourners out of empathy, rather than sympathy. He knows what they do not, and what they could not know: that Lazarus will be raised from the dead. Jesus's shed tears reveals to us that he has been moved to compassion. And one further note of significance is that this is the only instance in the New Testament when this Greek word, translated as the word *wept*, is used. Like many other instances when a Greek word is only used once in the New Testament, it draws us to acknowledge the particular significance of what is actually taking place. In this case, that significance is linked directly to the Samaritan's reaction to the victim. Lazarus, like the victim in this parable, is only half dead. This account of Jesus being moved with compassion and "raising Lazarus from his *sleep*" also presents us with a picture of what Jesus has come to do on our behalf.

Once moved with compassion, the Samaritan uses all of his available resources to provide immediate aid to the victim. And at this point, Jesus identifies another symbolic figure in this drama, the Samaritan's own beast. Some translations, such as the New International Version, describe it as a donkey. Whatever it was, it would have been a four-legged, creature, by definition, and also considered to be a beast of burden.[53] Again reminding us of what Jesus said he would do for us in Matthew 11:28–30: "Come to me, all you who are weary and burdened, and I will give you rest. Take my yoke upon you and learn from me, for I am gentle and humble in heart, and you will find rest for your souls. For my yoke is easy and my burden is light" (NIV).

Included in the resources that the Samaritan makes use of before placing the dying man on his own beast is oil and wine to clean the victim's wounds before he bandages them. Even these actions are significant in that they speak to what has been foreshadowed in Isaiah 53:5, which includes, in part, a description of the Messiah—"by his stripes we are healed"—which is also confirmed after the fact, in 1 Peter 2:24: "He himself bore our sins" in his body on the cross, so that we might die to sins and live for righteousness; "by his wounds (stripes in the KJV) you have been healed" (NIV).

Jesus, as compared to our state of being "half dead," becomes the victim of the same Jewish leaders who are responsible for not only beating and torturing Jesus before he is crucified—at which point he, too, could be considered to be physically half dead—but also robbing him of all dignity, signified by his own robe being removed. And in the same way the priest and the Levite when seeing the victim on the side of the road choose to pass him by, so do many of the Jewish leaders who see Jesus hanging on the cross, albeit understanding what condition he is in, remain void of compassion and consequently mock him, essentially passing him by on the other side of the road. Matthew 27:41–42 reads, "Likewise also the chief priests mocking him, with the scribes and elders, said, He saved others; himself he cannot save."

In Galatians 6:7, Paul tells the Galatians, "Be not deceived; God is not mocked: for whatsoever a man soweth, that shall he also reap." The priest and the Levite, when they pass the victim by on the other side of the road, are literally mocking God—as are we when we are likewise guilty of not loving our neighbor as ourselves. The key phrase in this warning to the Galatians is "Be not deceived." Our deception will always result in God being mocked. And this act of passing by the victim, as an act in which God is being mocked, is also symbolic of how many times Jesus, who is God, will be mocked, by Jew and Gentile alike, from the time he is arrested to the moment he gives up his ghost. In Matthew 27:29, after the Romans put a crown of thorns on Jesus's head, they bowed before him and "mocked him, saying Hail, King of the Jews!" Luke 18:32 reads, "For he shall be delivered unto the Gentiles, and shall be mocked, and spitefully entreated, and spitted on." Luke 22:63 tell us, "And the men that held Jesus mocked him and smote him." Then we discover in Luke 23:11, "And Herod with his men of war set him nought, and mocked him, and arrayed him in a gorgeous robe, and sent him again to Pilate." Luke 23:36 furthers this narrative, reading, "And the soldiers also mocked him, coming to him and offering him vinegar" (KJV).

Given this fact, that Jew and Gentile alike are guilty of crucifying Jesus, who is God, and mocking him in the process, both in word and in deed, this parable also becomes a foreshadowing of God, through the offering of Jesus's life, leveling the playing field for those who will be chosen by him to be saved—that is, those whom God will consider to be his chosen people will include everyone regardless of gender, nationality, ethnicity, age, or social, political, or economic standing. Galatians 3:28 reads, "There is neither Jew nor Greek, there is neither bond nor free, there is neither male nor female: for you are all one in Christ Jesus" (KJV). Essentially, in that there is no distinction between the ways that Jesus was mocked by both Jew and Gentile alike God will make no distinction when it comes to salvation, either.

The Samaritan, finally, after putting the victim on his beast, takes him to a place where he will be allowed the time to recuperate. It is no coincidence that this place is an inn. In essence, what the Samaritan does by his actions is to provide deliverance, redemption, and restoration to this victim, and by doing so he fulfills what it means to love God with his heart, mind, and soul, and to love his neighbor as himself.

The significance of the inn is really, at least, twofold. First, it represents our own need for recuperation, and what we might consider to be the sanctification process after we are given a new identity in Christ. Literally by his stripes, we have been healed from our fallen nature, and all deeds associated with it, which we inherited from the first Adam, as Colossians 3:9–11 makes plain: "Do not lie to each other, since you have taken off your old self with its practices and have put on the new self, which is being renewed in knowledge in the image of its creator. Here there is no Gentile or Jew, circumcised or uncircumcised, barbarian, Scythian, slave or free, but Christ is all, and is in all" (NIV).

Second, the inn reemphasizes Israel's own desolate condition and what Jesus, illustrated by all the Samaritan's provisions for the victim leading up to his carrying him to the inn, has done for us. At the time of Jesus's birth, there was no room for him to be born in the inn (Luke 2:7), symbolizing the fact that there was no room for him in all of Israel, from that moment and leading up to the time of his crucifixion. As the result of the sacrifice of Jesus's life, this world could be likened to an inn in that it is only a temporary place for us to stay while he goes to prepare a permanent place for us in his Father's house. As John 14:2–3 tells us, "In my Father's house are many mansions: if it were not so, I would have told you. I go to prepare a place for you. And if I go and prepare a place for you, I will come again, and receive you unto myself; that where I am, there you may be also" (KJV).

In the meantime, while we remain here in temporary residence, God has sent to us the Holy Spirit to be our Comforter. Thus, Jesus introduces the final character in the parable of the Good Samaritan, the host (or innkeeper, depending on the translation). The Greek word *pandocheus* simply means "an innkeeper, host."[54] Interestingly, the root word this word has been derived from is the Greek word *pandocheion*, which means "an inn, a public house for the reception of strangers."[55]

Ephesians 2:19 reads, "Now therefore you are no more strangers and foreigners, but fellow citizens with the saints, and of the household of God," which was touched on in chapter 24 (in paragraph 14) when discussing the account of Jesus's encounter with the Samaritan woman at the well. Now, in this parable, the Samaritan takes the victim to the inn to recuperate, the inn being by definition "a public house for the reception of strangers." The victim has been stripped almost completely bare, making it difficult to determine his station in life, as well as perhaps his ethnicity. It is obvious and important that Jesus has not given any other details to the lawyer concerning the man's identity because it shouldn't have mattered.

When the Samaritan takes this stranger to the inn, the inn not only symbolizes our temporary residence here on earth once we are betrothed to Jesus, but we are also given insight, first, into what God reveals to Peter when he is praying on the rooftop in Acts 10, later telling Cornelius, in verse 28, "You are well aware that it is against our law for a Jew to associate with or *visit* a Gentile. But God has shown me that I should not call anyone impure or unclean."

And second, we are given insight into what is also confirmed by Paul in the second chapter of the letter he wrote to the predominantly Gentile church in Ephesus, verses 11-16:

> "Therefore, remember that formerly you who are Gentiles by birth and called "uncircumcised" by those who call themselves "the circumcision" (which is done in the body by human hands)- remember that at that time you were separate from Christ, excluded from citizenship in Israel and foreigners to the covenants and promise, without hope and without God in the world. But now in Christ Jesus you who once were far away have been brought near by the blood of Christ. For he himself is our peace, who has made the two groups one and has destroyed the barrier, the dividing wall of hostility, by setting aside in his flesh the law with its commands and regulations. His purpose was to create in himself one new humanity out of the two, thus making peace, and in one body to reconcile both of them to God through the cross by which he put to death their hostility" (NIV).

In addition to Paul telling the Ephesians in this letter that God no longer makes a distinction between Jew and Gentile, and that whom he considers to be his chosen people now includes everyone he reveals himself to and accepts Jesus as Savior (verses 20 and 22). Paul also describes what the inn in this parable is meant to symbolize: "an holy temple in the Lord ... builded together for an habitation of God through the Spirit." In other words, it is nothing relating to brick and mortar constructed with human hands.

Like Jesus, the Samaritan in this parable holds no official religious office in Israel, yet he fulfills the role of both priest and Levite exemplified through all he does for the victim. This too is a critical point that Jesus is making here, but it is not necessarily one that is obvious, especially in the context of worship and what it is supposed to look like and include after Jesus is resurrected. Remembering, of course, that Jesus is our model in all things related to worship, because all things in him are meant to be received by God as worship, with the understanding that everything apart from this only serves to mock him.

As amazing as it might seem—but at this point, nothing might come as a surprise—Jesus's present and ongoing ministry, beginning with his resurrection, is represented in this parable through both the priest and the Levite, as well as the Samaritan. Perhaps not understood in this context, Hebrews 8:6 precisely addresses this point: "But now he has obtained a more excellent ministry, by as much as He is also the mediator of a better covenant, which has been enacted on better promises" (NASB).

The key to understanding this point is to know what the "more excellent ministry" is that Jesus has obtained through the offering of his life. And in order to know what this "more excellent ministry" actually is, it is necessary to look at the original Greek word used here and how it is meant to be understood in its biblical context.

The Greek word translated as the word *ministry* used in the above passage is *leitourgia*, which is where the word *liturgy* derives from. In a biblical context, this word means "a service of the priests relative to the prayers and sacrifices offered to God," and also "a gift or benefaction for the relief of the needy."[56] Jesus's present and ongoing "more excellent ministry" is literally that of priest and Levite.

In the parable of the Good Samaritan, Jesus could have had it be an interpreter of the law, a scribe, a Pharisee, or someone else who passed by on the other side of the road, but he didn't because he was making a much greater point, one that included what he came to do for us, as well as what our relationship with him would be like after his crucifixion—and all of this was in the context of worship. What the Samaritan does for the victim is precisely what Jesus came to do for us, which was being contrasted by what the actual priest and the Levite did not do, which consequently led to the half-dead condition of those entrusted to the care of the religious leaders in Israel.

Remember what Paul said in Galatians 6:7: "Be not deceived; God is not mocked: for whatsoever a man soweth, that shall he also reap." The priest and the Levite passing the victim by symbolizes what Israel has been sowing. And Jesus telling the Pharisees that their "house has been left unto them desolate" is his informing them of what they have reaped based on their sowing. The Samaritan, on the other hand, what he sows through his actions symbolizes Jesus visiting us in our condition of *spiritual widowhood*, with the result being that God breathes life into the church/bride, thus reviving her from her half-dead condition and granting her eternal life.

As has been maintained throughout *Spiritual Widowhood*, Jesus is our only model for what worship is supposed to look like. He also provides the reasons why. The word *leitourgia* is once again key to understanding not only what has been covered concerning Jesus's present and ongoing *"more excellent ministry"* as it relates to this parable, but also our own present and ongoing ministry, which is being demonstrated to us by the Samaritan in this parable. In the second paragraph of this chapter, I mentioned three points that Jesus was trying to make through the telling of this parable, and all three were in the context of worship. The first point revealed the "desolate condition" of Israel based on worship; the second point revealed what Jesus came to do to reverse this condition based on worship and revealed by the first point; and the third point was what worship, based on both the Samaritan's actions and the priest's and the Levite's inaction, was supposed to look like and to include going forward based on Jesus sacrificing his life for us, his bride.

No other place in the New Testament is this more clearly presented and confirmed than in Paul's letter to the church in Philippi. In Philippians 2:17, Paul writes, "Yea, and if I be offered upon the sacrifice and service of your faith, I joy, and rejoice with you all" (KJV). The word *service* used here is this same word, *leitourgia* that has been translated as the word *ministry* in Hebrews 6:8, previously discussed.

Paul is literally revealing in his letter to the Philippians that Jesus's "more excellent ministry" is also ours, that his present ministry is the combination of the ministries of both priest and Levite, and that he has served as our model for carrying out the combination of these same ministries. And by doing so, we fulfill what it means to love God with all of our being and our neighbors as ourselves. By not doing so, on the other hand, we are guilty of mocking God.

This reality is further clarified by Paul's inclusion of the word *sacrifice* in conjunction with the word *service* to indicate the necessity to include both in the demonstration of our faith. The word *sacrifice* used here also happens to be the same Greek word translated as the word *sacrifice* used in Romans 12:1, which tells us that we are to be living and holy sacrifices, as well as the word for *sacrifice* in Hebrews 10:2: "But this man (Jesus), after he had offered one sacrifice for sins forever, sat down on the right hand of God" (KJV).

The Greek word translated as the word *sacrifice* in all three of the above passages is *thysia*, which means "sacrifice, victim—the act or the victim, literally or figuratively."[57] This means that as "living and holy sacrifices," we are all, as Jesus both has modeled and remains for us, to be both priest and Levite. And for those who shepherd us today and must give an account for us, they are the ones, by virtue of their leadership positions, who bear the greatest responsibility not just for telling us what we should be doing inside the church but also, and more importantly, leading the way for us outside of the church, where the worship field, through the offering up of acts of mercy and compassion, remains level and where we are all equally called to bear Christ's reproach.

And as was touched on earlier concerning who the victim in this parable represents, it is not only those whom Jesus came to deliver, redeem, and restore, but also Jesus himself. Given that the Greek word for *sacrifice*, discussed in the previous paragraph, based on the root word it is derived from, means "the act of sacrifice and/or the victim of sacrifice," Jesus models both for us. He willingly offers up his own life for us, but in doing so he becomes the victim of his own sacrifice. Therefore, Jesus is represented in this parable by both the Samaritan, who is offering up to God a deed offering (sacrifice) by helping the victim, and the victim, himself, who has been beaten, robbed, and left for dead—which, is what we see happening to Jesus after he is arrested. He is falsely accused, beaten, tortured, humiliated, and then nailed to a cross, where he dies. Jesus is thus both the act of sacrifice and the victim of sacrifice.

Hopefully now, based on everything that has been covered in this chapter up to this point in the context of what it means to be "living sacrifices holy and acceptable to God, which is our spiritual service of worship," new insights and understanding have been provided regarding the reasons that Jesus included all that he did in this parable. I also hope that the meaning of passages like 2 Corinthians 9:12 that Paul wrote to the church in Corinth will become even more profound regarding what it means to daily live out our lives as "living and holy sacrifices." This particular passage Paul writes after giving the Corinthians more than ample reason and encouragement for being generous in their giving to others, just as God has been generous to them. He then tells what the outcomes will be: "This service [*leitourgia*] that you perform is not only supplying the needs of the Lord's people but is also overflowing in many expressions of thanks [*eucharistia*] to God" (NIV).

And finally, after telling this parable to the lawyer, Jesus once again asks the lawyer a question in response to the question that prompted Jesus to tell this parable in the first place. We see this new question in Luke 10:36: "Which of these three do you think was a neighbor to the man who fell into the hands of robbers"(NIV)?

Whether the lawyer has realized it or not, Jesus, in the telling of this parable, has inferred that there is no difference between the thieves who attacked and left the victim for dead (half dead) and the priest and the Levite who passed him by leaving him for dead (half dead). He is saying that the lawyer's guilt, given that he is a religious leader in Israel, is equal to the guilt of the priest and the Levite.

The lawyer's response to Jesus's second question appears to be correct based on Jesus's response of, "Go and do likewise," but what it does not do is give us any further insight into whether the lawyer acknowledged his own guilt (as a result of understanding what Jesus was really confronting him with through the telling of this parable) and repented, the latter meaning that the lawyer's newly expanded view regarding whom his neighbor should include in God's eyes, in the context of worship led him to act. All we are really certain of is that the lawyer knew the right answer based on the one he gives in Luke 10:37: "He that showed mercy on him." This answer that the lawyer gave in response to Jesus's second question has become in recent years, according to some interpretations of this parable, the scriptural basis for churches to undertake and carry out ministries of mercy.

To really understand what the lawyer's answer in this parable is meant to be connected to, though, you have to go back to the first question he asked Jesus: "What must I do to inherit eternal life?" Jesus answers that question with the question, "How do you interpret the law?" The lawyer correctly answers, "To love God with your heart, mind, and soul, and to love your neighbor as yourself." Jesus already knows that this lawyer knows the correct answer for what he must do in order to inherit eternal life, as well as the fact that that there is no evidence in the lawyer's life to show that he fulfills either of these two things. Plainly stated, the evidence for those who love God with their hearts, minds and souls as well as love their neighbors as themselves will be recognized and known for their acts/offerings of mercy and compassion, especially when they are personally being carried out by us for the least of these among us.

The evidence that a person does these two things is, of course, his or her *worship-driven life* surrendered to acts of compassion and mercy benefitting the least of those amongst us. Why is this so? Because of "God's mercies we are to be living and holy sacrifices which is our spiritual service of worship." So, for all of us who confess Jesus as Savior and Bridegroom, the worship field is level when it comes to showing mercy and compassion. No one is exempt, regardless of one's station(s) in life, both inside and outside of the church. Therefore, to interpret what Jesus tells the lawyer at the end of this parable, "Go and do likewise," as being the scriptural basis for churches to undertake and carry out ministries of mercy reveals, perhaps, that such churches have no more understanding of what worshipping God in spirit and in truth looks like than this interpreter of the law does.

I would like to make one last observation before ending this chapter. It is doubtful that the outcome with the interpreter of the law, after Jesus tells him to go and do likewise, in any way resembled that of the Samaritan woman at the well. If the outcome for the lawyer had been similar, then we can be fairly certain that it would have been recorded at the end of this account. The fact that it wasn't undoubtedly makes Jesus's encounter with the Samaritan woman, and the subsequent outcome, all the more profound.

Chapter 26: Endings and Beginnings

In Genesis 2:2, we read that after six days of creation, God rests on the seventh day. Genesis 2:7-8 reads, "Then the Lord God creates man from the dust of the earth ... and puts him in a garden he planted eastward of Eden." And finally in Genesis 2:15, we learn that God's purpose for this man called Adam he puts in the garden is "to dress it and to keep it." thus begins our beginnings, and the purpose of our beginnings, which is worship.

After Adam and Eve commit an act of self-worship (adultery/ idolatry), we read in Genesis 3:24, "God drove out the man ... and blocks the way back into the garden of Eden by placing Cherubims, and a flaming sword which turned every way, to keep the way of the tree of life" (KJV). Because Adam failed "to dress and to keep" the garden as God had instructed him to do, allowing deception to enter in through the Serpent, God's order that we worship was corrupted, thus ending our beginnings in a setting that was previously void of sin.

Adam and Eve, considered to be one flesh in their relationship to God as husband and wife, are literally divorced by him because of their act of adultery. In this, they embody the first condition of *spiritual widowhood*. Consequently, they bring this same condition as a new beginning for all humankind.

God does not abandon Adam and Eve, though, to what could be described as a place of desolation given both the physical setting they are now in and their spiritual condition. Instead, he pursues them as a hopeful bridegroom would pursue a prospective bride, promising to send his own Son as an offering for us, whose sacrifice of his own life would ensure our entry back into the garden and, thus, a new beginning.

Therefore, the physical condition of widowhood and fatherlessness becomes the clearest evidence for all generations after Adam and Eve not only of the consequence, namely, that all humankind has been made to suffer because of their adulterous act of self-worship, but also of our own need for deliverance, redemption, and restoration. And for those who believe that Jesus is the promised Son of God sent by his Father to be the onetime sacrificial offering to atone for our inherited sin, and the only one who can take away our spiritual conditions of widowhood and fatherlessness, there is hope.

And based on the hope that we have in this promise to one day be joined together with Jesus back in the/a garden whose entryway is until then blocked, is it any wonder that Jesus was arrested in a garden (Matthew 26:36–56)? And although some dispute that the place where Jesus was crucified was a garden, there is no apparent dispute that the place where he was buried was a garden. John 19:41 reads, "Now the place where he was crucified there was a garden; and in the garden a new sepulcher." That Jesus was buried in a garden also means that he was resurrected in that same garden. He was, in fact, even mistaken by Mary Magdalene to be a gardener. John 20:15 reads, "Thinking he [Jesus] was the gardener, She [Mary Magdalene] said, 'Sir, if you have carried him away, tell me where you have put him, and I will get him'" (NIV). Just as an aside, it should also be noted that Mary Magdalene was the first evangelist. Remaining at the empty tomb after the disciples left she was not only the first to witness the resurrected Jesus, but she was also the first to report (deliver) the good news of the Gospel to the disciples; that Jesus had been resurrected from the dead.

In Revelation 21:2, we are even given a description of the paradise reserved for us: "And I John saw the holy city, new Jerusalem, coming down from God out of heaven, prepared as a bride adorned for her husband." Then skipping ahead to Revelation 22:1–2, we learn, "And he showed me a pure river of water of life, clear as crystal, proceeding out of the throne of God and of the Lamb. In the midst of the street of it, and on either side of the river, was there the tree of life, which bare twelve manner of fruits, and yielded her fruit every month: and the leaves of the tree were for the healing of the nations."

Notwithstanding the fact that the word *garden* is not used anywhere in this description of the New Jerusalem, is there any disputing, given that it is unmistakably the place where the tree of life has been placed and given that the precedent for its original placement was in a garden, that a garden is what is being described in Revelation 21:1–2?

In effect, just as Adam's purpose was "to dress and to keep" the garden, making him a gardener, we, likewise, are to be gardeners. And like the first Adam in the garden, and like Jesus as the last Adam, we are the Lord's gardeners, and our purpose, like theirs, is to worship God through word (giving thanks to God in all things) and deed (that which we do unto the least of these), which is what it means for us today "to dress it and to keep it." Especially important here is "visiting the widow and the fatherless in their distress."

And if we will devote ourselves to worshipping God in these ways, he promises us, perhaps more plainly in Isaiah 58:10–12 than in any other place in scripture, that if we will "spend ourselves in behalf of the hungry and satisfy the needs of the oppressed," the outcome will be as follows:

> Then your light will rise in the darkness, and night will become like the noonday. The Lord will guide you always; he will satisfy your needs in a sun-scorched land and will strengthen your frame. *You will be like a well-watered garden, like a spring whose waters never fail.* Your people will rebuild the ancient ruins and will raise up the age-old foundations; you will be called Repairer of Broken Walls, Restorer of Streets and Dwellings (NIV, emphasis added).

The first time that God actually issues a warning to Israel not to cause harm to "any widow, or fatherless child" is in Exodus 22:22. In the two verses that follow, God tells the Israelites that if they are caused any harm whatsoever and if they even so much as whimper (obviously my phraseology; the Bible's is "they cry at all unto me"), he will hear their cry, and those who are responsible for their suffering "I will kill you with the sword; and your own wives shall be widows, and your children fatherless."

It is important to remember that doing nothing at all, passing by on the other side of the road, not only makes us just as guilty of causing harm as if we had intentionally sought to do so but also makes us guilty of mocking God. Caring for the widows and the fatherless is the responsibility of each of us, and there is no one aside from us, either individually, corporately, or governmentally, to point the finger of blame at for not being faithful to do so. As my wife, Gloria, is fond of reminding me every time I point a finger at someone else, there are always three fingers pointing back at me.

We can never be reminded enough that just as Jesus came to serve/minister and not be served/ministered to, we as his betrothed, as gardeners in the Lord's garden, as both priest and Levite, are compelled to do likewise.

In the upper room the night Jesus was betrayed, before he serves the Passover meal, he washes the feet of his disciples. In John 13:8, after Peter tells Jesus that he will never allow the latter to wash his feet, Jesus tells Peter that if he does not allow him to do this, he will "have no part in him." Jesus, as God, had no equals on earth. By washing the disciples' feet, that is, serving and not being served, he did unto them what they could not likewise do unto him. But they could, by his example, serve those who were not in a position to do unto them likewise. It's almost as if Jesus is saying to Peter when the latter tells the former that he can't wash his feet, especially given the fact that Peter, in Matthew 16, is the one who correctly recognizes Jesus as the Christ, that Peter, in not letting Jesus wash his feet, really doesn't know who Jesus is or understand what is going on.

In the same way, when we who have been made holy through the righteousness of Jesus and the indwelling of the Holy Spirit are unwilling to serve those who cannot serve us back in like manner because of our respective positions in the church, in society, etc., Jesus has no part in us.

No wonder Jesus says in Matthew 19:24, "It is easier for a camel to go through the eye of a needle, than for a rich man to enter into the kingdom of God." And in James 1:10-11 and 2:5-6, he does not pull any punches either when he speaks of the rich.

James 1:10–11 reads, "But the rich should take pride in their humiliation – since they will pass away like a wild flower. For the sun rises with scorching heat and withers the plant; its blossom falls and its beauty is destroyed. In the same way, the rich will fade away even while they go about their business" (NIV).

James 2:5–6 reads, "Listen, my dear brothers and sisters: Has not God chosen those who are poor in the eyes of the world to be rich in faith and to inherit the kingdom he promised those who love him? But you have dishonored the poor. Is it not the rich who are exploiting you? Are they not the ones who are dragging you into court" (NIV)?

Finally, if there is any question as to the likelihood of the rich entering into the kingdom of God, James leaves no room for doubt based on his words in 5:1–7:

> Now listen, you rich people, weep and wail because of the misery that is coming on you. Your wealth has rotted, and moths have eaten your clothes. Your gold and silver are corroded. Their corrosion will testify against you and eat your flesh like fire. You have hoarded wealth in the last days. Look! The wages you failed to pay the workers who mowed your fields are crying out against you. The cries of the harvesters have reached the ears of the Lord Almighty. You have lived on earth in luxury and self-indulgence. You have fattened yourselves in the day of the slaughter. You have condemned and murdered the innocent one, who was not opposing you. Be patient, then brothers and sisters, until the Lord's coming. See how the farmer waits for

> the land to yield its valuable crop, patiently waiting for
> the autumn and spring rains (NIV).

The rich might also include those individuals who have more privilege, whether by virtue of being born into a majority culture and/ or being born into a wealthy family, or corporations such as a church community that enjoys more privilege than other church communities because of wealth and cultural advantage. The greater burden will always be on those such as these for modeling Christ's example of "serving and not being served," especially serving those who will never be able to return the favor.

Again, how can it be possible, as James tells us in the first lines of chapter 4, verse 8, for us to draw near to God so that he will draw near to us if we are only willing to draw near to those who are most like us and who are able to return our favors? If you will remember, Jesus's criteria for separating the sheep and the goats in Matthew 25:40 are based on a very personal "you": "That *you* have done this unto the least of these, that *you* have done this unto me."

In that the title of this concluding chapter is "Endings and Beginnings," it seems appropriate to end with three questions that might lead to new beginnings. The first question to consider is, based on the material that has been covered in Spiritual Widowhood, have we, today, as the betrothed of Jesus fallen prey to the subtleties of deception, just as Eve was deceived by the Serpent, that has caused our minds to be corrupted away from "our sincere and pure devotion to Christ" (NIV)? If so, why? If not, why?

If the conclusion reached for our answer to the first question is that we believe, as the church, that we have fallen prey to the subtleties of deception in the same way that Eve was deceived by the Serpent, then the second question we should consider is: To what extent do we think that we have been deceived? Do we think that our deception has reached such critical mass proportions as to cause the abomination of desolation to be standing where it should not be, i.e., in our midst as the church? If so, why? If not, why?

And finally, if we believe that, first, the subtleties of deception have taken root in the church, and second, that this deception has reached critical mass proportions, then are we, either individually or corporately, willing to surrender *ourselves*, regardless of the cost, and based on Jesus's own life example for what it really means and looks like to be "a living sacrifice, holy and acceptable to God, which is our reasonable service of worship, exemplified through "the giving of thanks in all things" (loving God with all your heart, mind and soul), and serving the least of these among us (loving our neighbors as ourselves), so that we might be the *"pure and undefiled bride"* that God desires us to be *"chaste as a virgin?"*

On the other hand, if the conclusions reached for these first 2 questions is no, then it would seem befitting to conclude Spiritual Widowhood by reminding ourselves of the prophet Hosea's exhortation to Israel, in chapter 10 verse 12, for returning to the ways of the Lord, followed by his description of their guilt and what the resulting consequences would be in 10:13-14:

> Sow righteousness for yourselves, reap the fruit of unfailing love, and break up your unplowed ground; for it is time to seek the Lord, until he comes and showers his righteousness on you. But you have planted wickedness, you have reaped evil, you have eaten the fruit of *deception.* Because you have depended on your own strength and on your many warriors, the roar of battle will rise against your people, so that all your fortresses will be devastated".... (NIV, emphasis added).

Addendum

I n 1989, 2 years after starting The Chattanooga Widows Ministry (later changed to Widows Harvest Ministries) under New City Fellowship church in Chattanooga, TN, an article was published about this ministry in the July/August issue of the "PCA Messenger." Included was a sidebar article written by A. Randy Nabors, pastor of New City Fellowship, entitled, *Help The Widows*! The following is Randy's article, quoted in its entirety, as a final plea for the necessity of God's people "to visit the widow and the fatherless in their distress" so that we might truly be the "pure and undefiled" bride that God desires us to be.

Help The Widows!

If there were only something specific we could do to help the poor – some kind of ministry that would reach those people truly in need and get church members directly and personally involved. A ministry that would give practical help but also would be evangelistic, clearly holding up the name of Jesus and His work on Calvary. What is more, a work that would enable the people helped to become workers too – having a ministry of their own. Could there be such a work with a strong biblical mandate? Could there be a work among the poor that would show clear results and definite change? Could there be such a work which a local church like ours could do without losing our people to various para-church organizations?

Yes, there could be, and is, such a work; praise the Lord! The

Chattanooga Widows Ministry clearly answers the concerns raised above. I have been involved with inner-city ministry all the years I have been preaching. The poor have always been a concern of mine. For the most part, the years went by with very little identifiable change in people's lives. And then along came widows. Actually, they had been there all the time – they were just invisible to me. I did not see them except as old ladies who lived in the city. I had youth groups, but I never thought about a widows group. To be honest, taking care of old people never seemed like an exciting idea, but God has His own excitement waiting for those who are obedient. There are widows in every city and town for an adventure like this. There are Christians in every congregation looking for an opportunity like this.

What we have here in Chattanooga are ladies who are struggling every day to stay alive, well and cheerful in spite of poverty, loneliness and sickness. No one sees any use for them – sometimes not even their own children. Then a missionary, like Andy Mendonsa, meets them and invites them to join a group of other widows who pray – and pray with power and effectiveness. He introduces the widow to a church that cares, fixes her roof, repairs her plumbing, gets her into a hospital or nursing home – if it is needed, visits her and loves her. And the church finds someone who is not "manipulating the system," who receives even a little help with joy and gratitude. Some of these ladies even start coming to church – even though we "soft sell" the idea. They just like coming and being with people who like them.

Now that is not a bad idea for a ministry. How amazing that the Bible prescribed it long ago; and this "cutting edge," inner-city ministry finally caught up with what God had in mind all along! Help the widows! I recommend that all God's people investigate this ministry, copy it and do it themselves. [58]
- A. Randy Nabors, New City Fellowship, Chattanooga, TN

Notes

1   John MacArthur, *Caring for Widows*, (Chicago, IL: Moody Press, 1991), 12.

2   *Strong's Greek Lexicon* (KJV), G5503, s.v. "chēra," *Blue Letter Bible*, accessed July 20, 2016, www.blueletterbible.org//lang/lexicon/lexicon.cfm?Strongs=G5503&t=KJV.

3   *Strong's Hebrew Lexicon* (KJV), H490, s.v. "'almanah," *Blue Letter Bible*, accessed July 20, 2016, www.blueletterbible.org//lang/lexicon/lexicon.cfm?Strongs=H490&t=KJV.

4   John MacArthur, *Caring for Widows*, (Chicago: Moody Press, 1991), 33.

5   *The Free Dictionary*, s.v. "legal precedent," accessed October 4, 2016, http://www.thefreedictionary.com/Legal+precedent.

6   *Strong's Hebrew Lexicon* (KJV), H1644, s.v. "garash," accessed July 20, 2016, www.blueletterbible.org//lang/lexicon/lexicon.cfm?Strongs=H1644&t=KJV.

7   *Strong's Greek Lexicon* (KJV), G2356, s.v. "thrēskeia," www.blueletterbible.org//lang/lexicon/lexicon.cfm?Strongs=G2356&t=KJV.

8   Ibid., G4352, s.v. "proskyneō," accessed July 13, 2016, www.blueletterbible.org//lang/lexicon/lexicon.cfm?Strongs=G4352&t=KJV.

9   *Strong's Hebrew Lexicon* (KJV), H7812, s.v. "shachah," accessed July 20, 2016, www.blueletterbible.org//lang/lexicon/lexicon.cfm?Strongs=H7812&t=KJV.

10   Ibid., H5647, s.v. "'abad," accessed July 12, 2016, www.blueletterbible.org//lang/lexicon/lexicon.cfm?Strongs=H5647&t=KJV.

11 *Strong's Greek Lexicon* (KJV), G2999, "latreia," accessed July 12, 2016, www.blueletterbible.org//lang/lexicon/lexicon.cfm?Strongs=G2999&t=KJV.

12 Ibid., G283, s.v. "amiantos," accessed July 20, 2016, www.blueletterbible.org//lang/lexicon/lexicon.cfm?Strongs=G283&t=KJV.

13 *Online Etymology Dictionary*, s.v. "asbestos," accessed October 4, 2016, http://www.etymonline.com/index.php?term=asbestos.

14 Dr. Amy Sherman, *Sharing God's Heart for the Poor* (Charlottesville, VA: Trinity Presbyterian Church, 2000), 18–21.

15 Ibid., 18.

16 Ibid.

17 *Strong's Greek Lexicon* (KJV), G2048, s.v. "erēmos," accessed July 12, 2016, www.blueletterbible.org//lang/lexicon/lexicon.cfm?Strongs=G2048&t=KJV.

18 MacArthur, *Caring for Widows*, (Chicago: Moody Press, 1991), 12.

19 *Strong's Hebrew Lexicon* (KJV), G2050, s.v. "erēmōsis," accessed July 20, 2016, www.blueletterbible.org//lang/lexicon/lexicon.cfm?Strongs=G2050&t=KJV.

20 Ibid., H490, s.v. "'almanah," accessed July 20, 2016, www.blueletterbible.org//lang/lexicon/lexicon.cfm?Strongs=H490&t=KJV.

21 *Strong's Greek Lexicon* (KJV), G1135, s.v. "gynē," accessed July 20, 2016, www.blueletterbible.org//lang/lexicon/lexicon.cfm?Strongs=G1135&t=KJV.

22 Ibid., G5310, s.v. "hypsistos," www.blueletterbible.org//lang/lexicon/lexicon.cfm?Strongs=G5310&t=KJV.

23 Ibid., G5272, s.v. "hypokrisis," accessed July 4, 2016, www.blueletterbible.org//lang/lexicon/lexicon.cfm?Strongs=G5272&t=KJV.

24 Ibid., G701, s.v. "arestos," accessed July 4, 2016, www.blueletterbible.org//lang/lexicon/lexicon.cfm?Strongs=G701&t=KJV.

25 Acts 6 (KJV): "And in those days when," *Blue Letter Bible*, accessed July 4, 2016, www.blueletterbible.org//kjv/act/6/1/t_conc_1024004.

26 *Strong's Greek Lexicon* (KJV), G3737, s.v. "orphanos," accessed July 7, 2016, www.blueletterbible.org//lang/lexicon/lexicon.cfm?Stro.ngs=G3737&t=KJV.

27 "Young's Literal Translation," *Wikipedia*, accessed October 4, 2016, https://en.wikipedia.org/wiki/Young%27s_Literal_Translation.

28 "Darby Bible," *Wikipedia*, accessed October 4, 2016, https://en.wikipedia.org/wiki/Darby_Bible.

29 Proverbs 21:2 (NASB): "Every man's way is right," *Blue Letter Bible*, accessed July 8, 2016, www.blueletterbible.org//nasb/pro/21/2/s_649002.

30 *Strong's Greek Lexicon* (KJV), G5083, s.v. "tēreō," accessed July 8, 2016, www.blueletterbible.org//lang/lexicon/lexicon.cfm?Strongs=G5083&t=KJV.

31 *Strong's Greek Lexicon* (KJV), H8104. s.v. "shamar," accessed Nov 12, 2016, www.blueletterbible.org//lang/lexicon/lexicon.cfm?Strongs=H8104&t=KJV

32 *Strong's Greek Lexicon* (KJV), G5083, s.v. "tēreō," accessed July 8, 2016, www.blueletterbible.org//lang/lexicon/lexicon.cfm?Strongs=G5083&t=KJV.

33 Hilary of Poitiers – Against the Arians of Auxentius of Milan xii (mpl 10.616) quoted from Calvin's Insititutes, "The Prefatory Address to King Francis," in *Institutes of the Christian Religion*, Book 1, (Westminister, PA:, Library of Christian Classics, 1960).

34 Ibid.

35 "Constantine the Great and Christianity," *Wikipedia*, accessed October 4, 2016, https://en.wikipedia.org/wiki/Constantine_the_Great_and_Christianity.

36 "Statistics of incarcerated African-American males," *Wikipedia*, accessed October 4, 2016, https://en.wikipedia.org/wiki/Statistics_of_incarcerated_African-American_males.

37 "America's Changing Religious Landscape," *PewResearchCenter*, May 12, 2015, www.pewforum.org/2015/05/12/americas-changing-religious-landscape/.

38 Anna Rappaport, "Facts about Women, Old Age, and Retirement," October 2014, *Society of Actuaries*, soa.org/Files/Research/Projects/

Research-2014-impact-risk-woman-report.pdf, accessed October 5, 2016.

39   Ibid.

40   *Strong's Greek Lexicon* (KJV), G2999, s.v. "latreia," accessed July 12, 2016, www.blueletterbible.org//lang/lexicon/lexicon. cfm?Strongs=G2999&t=KJV.

41   Ibid., H5647, "'abad," www.blueletterbible.org//lang/lexicon/lexicon.cfm?Strongs=H5647&t=KJV.

42   Romans 12 (NASB): "Therefore I urge you brethren," *Blue Letter Bible*, accessed July 12, 2016, www.blueletterbible.org//nasb/rom/12/1/s_1058001.

43   Ibid G2048, s.v. "erēmos," *Blue Letter Bible*, www.blueletterbible.org//lang/lexicon/lexicon.cfm?Strongs=G2048&t=KJV.

44   Ibid., G4352, s.v. "proskyneō," accessed July 13, 2016, www.blueletterbible.org//lang/lexicon/lexicon.cfm?Strongs=G4352&t=KJV.

45   Ibid., H5647, s.v. "'abad," www.blueletterbible.org//lang/lexicon/lexicon.cfm?Strongs=H5647&t=KJV.

46   Ibid., G4353, s.v. "proskynētēs," accessed July 13, 2016, www.blueletterbible.org//lang/lexicon/lexicon.cfm?Strongs=G4353&t=KJV.

47   Fritz Rienecker and Cleon Rogers, *Linguistic Key to the Greek New Testament*, (Grand Rapids, MI: The Zondervan Corporation, 1976, 1980), 719.

48   *Strong's Greek Lexicon* (KJV), G2168, s.v. "eucharisteō," accessed November 21, 2016, www.blueletterbible.org//lang/lexicon/lexicon.cfm?Strongs=G2168&t=KJV.

49   *Strong's Greek Lexicon* (KJV), G1344, s.v. "dikaioō," accessed July 14, 2016, www.blueletterbible.org//lang/lexicon/lexicon.cfm?Strongs=G1344&t=KJV.

50   "What to Expect at a Shiva," *Kveller,* accessed October 6, 2016, www.kveller.com/article/what-to-expect-at-a-shiva/.

51   *Strong's Greek Lexicon* (KJV), G2799, s.v. "klaiō," accessed July 16, 2016, www.blueletterbible.org//lang/lexicon/lexicon.cfm?Strongs=G2799&t=KJV.

52 *Strong's Greek Lexicon* (KJV), G1145, s.v. "dakryō," accessed July 16, 2016, www.blueletterbible.org//lang/lexicon/lexicon. cfm?Strongs=G1145&t=KJV.

53 *Strong's Greek Lexicon* (KJV), G2934, s.v. "ktēnos," accessed November 21, 2016, www.blueletterbible.org//lang/lexicon/ lexicon.cfm?Strongs=G2934&t=KJV.

54 Ibid., G3830, s.v. "pandocheus," accessed July 18, 2016, www. blueletterbible.org//lang/lexicon/lexicon.cfm?Strongs =G3830&t=KJV.

55 Ibid., G3829, s.v. "pandocheion," www.blueletterbible.org//lang/ lexicon/lexicon.cfm?Strongs=G3829&t=KJV.

56 Ibid., G3009, s.v. "leitourgia," accessed July 16, 2016, www.blueletterbible.org//lang/lexicon/lexicon. cfm?Strongs=G3009&t=KJV.

57 Ibid., G2378, s.v. "thysia," www.blueletterbible.org//lang/lexicon/ lexicon.cfm?Strongs=G2378&t=KJV.

58 A. Randy Nabors, *Help The Widows!*, Lawrenceville, Ga; PCA Messenger, July-August 1989), 14. Reprinted in its entirety by permission of John Dunahoo, Business Administrator, PCA Christian Education and Publications, 1700 North Brown Road, Lawrenceville, GA 30043, June 27, 2014

About the Author

Andy Mendonsa and his wife Gloria live in the historic neighborhood of St Elmo with their 2 dogs; Fergus, a Welsh Corgi, and Thumper, a Basset Hound. Founded in 1885 and located at the foot of Lookout Mountain in Chattanooga, Tennessee they have resided in this diverse urban neighborhood since 1985. Andy continues to serve as servant Director of Widows Harvest Ministries the ministry he helped found in 1987.

Made in the USA
Columbia, SC
06 January 2021

30410218R00105